SACRED UNION: EXPLORING THE SPIRITUAL DIMENSIONS OF SEX AND ITS IMPACT ON THE SOUL.

First edition. February 13, 2024.

Copyright © 2024 Sophia Mcintyre.

ISBN: 979-8224266104

Written by Sophia Mcintyre.

Sacred Union

"Exploring the Spiritual Dimensions of Sex and Its Impact on the Soul"

I. INTRODUCTION

Sex is often viewed as a time of physical pleasure and often or not a few look beyond the surface lust it offers; most people believe that they are completely unaffected by the deeper consequences that lay beneath the surface. If only they took keen notice, they would note a shift in their temperaments and physical bodies.

So, what then is the connection between spirituality and sexuality? Could it be responsible for most of the destructive experiences faced in life both in the flesh and psychosomatically?

The notion that S.T.D's and uninvited pregnancies are the only negatives consequences of having sex is often far-fetched? A rapid Google search on 'Sex or Sexual Intercourse'; Freedictionary, Merriam Webster to even Oxford Dictionaries - they all give a similar definition of "union between a male and a female...", "process by which sperm from the male is deposited ..." and "Sexual contact between individuals involving penetration......

Most folks have a basic idea of what sex is. The Bible defines sex as two becoming one; **Mark 10: 8** states *"and the two will become one flesh.'* During a sexual encounter there is accurately a 'union' and the two individuals involved are 'joined' to 'become "ONE". This what we define as a *"sacred union",* this is where as the bible declares; 'two' are joined to 'one'.

A. Brief Overview of the Book

Sacred Union: "Exploring the Spiritual Dimensions of Sex and Its Impact on the Soul" delves into the intricate interplay between sexuality and spirituality. This enlightening exploration unveils the spiritual essence of sex, examining its positive and negative consequences on each individual's spiritual journey. The book navigates through the sacred connections found in various spiritual traditions, unraveling the transformative potential of intimate connections. It carefully addresses both the positive aspects of spiritual intimacy and the potential distortions that may arise. By offering insights, practices, and tools, this book guides readers in cultivating mindful and sacred sexuality, harmonizing the physical and spiritual realms. Ultimately, it encourages a balanced and reverent approach to sexuality, fostering personal growth, emotional connection, and a deeper alignment with the divine. "Sacred Union" is a beacon for those seeking to understand and honor the spiritual dimensions of sex on their profound journey toward enlightenment and connection.

In "Sacred Union," readers make a deliberate choice to embark on a journey that goes beyond the physical aspects of sex, exploring the spiritual nuances that often remain veiled in the dark corners of hushed tone and taboo conversations. The book not only uncovers the positive consequences of spiritual intimacy, such as fostering emotional and energetic bonds and supporting personal growth, but also courageously examines into the potential negative consequences, offering insights into how spiritual distortions can impact mental and emotional well-being.

With a balanced approach, the book provides practical tools for navigating challenges, encouraging readers to look beyond the normal, recognize and address spiritual disconnects while offering transformative approaches to overcome obstacles. It puts emphasis on the importance of mindful and sacred sexuality, guiding readers in harmonizing their physical and spiritual energies. Throughout the chapters, the book weaves together wisdom from various spiritual traditions, presenting rituals, ceremonies, and practices that help individuals align their intimate connections with divine principles.

"Sacred Union" serves as a compass for those seeking to embrace divine wisdom in their relationships, and at the same time incorporating spiritual principles into their daily lives. The book culminates in a call to uphold reverence for the sacred essence of sex, inspiring positive transformations that echo not only in individual lives but also in the broader tapestry of interconnected spiritual journeys, especially where an individual has or had multiple sexual partners.

In the concluding chapters of "Sacred Union," the book extends an invitation to readers to embrace a profound integration of divine wisdom into their daily lives. It underscores the transformative power of practices such as meditation, prayer, and rituals, providing tangible tools for fostering spiritual growth within intimate connections. By encouraging a holistic approach, the book offers insights into harmonizing physical desires with spiritual principles, ultimately fostering a balanced and sacred existence.

Throughout, the narrative maintains a compassionate tone, recognizing the complexity of human experiences and relationships. It emphasizes the importance of seeking guidance and support when navigating challenges related to spiritual disconnect, ensuring that readers feel empowered and equipped to embark on their own transformative journeys.

In its entirety, "Sacred Union" serves as a guide for those who are ready to explore the spiritual dimensions of sex with curiosity, reverence, and a commitment to personal and collective growth. It is an empowering resource for individuals seeking to deepen their understanding of the sacred connection between sexuality and spirituality, providing both insights and practical guidance for navigating this intricate and transformative terrain.

B. Importance of Exploring the Spiritual Dimensions of Sex.

Exploring the spiritual dimensions of sex holds significant importance for individuals on their personal and collective journeys. Here are key reasons why examining into the spiritual aspects of sexuality is meaningful:

1. **Deepening Intimate Connections:** Understanding the spiritual dimensions of sex can enhance the depth and meaning of intimate connections. It allows individuals to approach sexuality with reverence, fostering a sense of sacredness and connection within relationships.

2. **Personal Growth and Transformation:** Exploring the spiritual aspects of sex provides an avenue for personal growth and transformation. It invites individuals to examine their beliefs, values, and attitudes towards sexuality, encouraging a journey of self-discovery and self-improvement.

3. **Harmonizing Body and Spirit:** Integrating spirituality into sexuality offers a holistic approach, harmonizing the physical and spiritual aspects of human existence. This balance contributes to a more integrated and aligned sense of self.

4. **Cultivating Mindful Sexuality:** Spiritual exploration encourages mindful sexuality, where individuals engage in intimate connections with heightened awareness, honesty, presence, and intention. This mindfulness can lead to deeper, richer, more meaningful experiences.

5. **Fostering Emotional and Energetic Bonds:** Identifying the spiritual dimensions of sex can deepen emotional and energetic bonds

between partners. It goes beyond the physical act, allowing for a profound connection on emotional, energetic, and spiritual levels.

6. **Addressing Negative Consequences:** Understanding the potential negative consequences of spiritual distortions in sexuality enables individuals to address challenges proactively. It provides a framework for navigating difficulties and seeking positive transformations.

7. **Contributing to Collective Consciousness:** As people explore and embrace the spiritual dimensions of sex, it contributes to a broader shift in collective consciousness. It fosters a cultural awareness that recognizes the sacred nature of intimate connections, promoting healthier attitudes towards sexuality.

8. **Enhancing Relationships with the Divine:** The exploration of spiritual dimensions in sex offers an opportunity to enhance one's relationship with the divine or the sacred. It becomes a path for spiritual seekers to connect with a higher purpose and transcendental aspects of existence.

9. **Surpassing Cultural Stigmas**: By diving into the spiritual dimensions of sex, individuals can challenge and rise above cultural stigmas surrounding sexuality. It encourages open conversations, breaking taboos, and fostering a more inclusive and accepting societal attitude towards diverse expressions of intimacy.

10. **Encouraging Consent and Respect:** A spiritual exploration of sex often emphasizes the importance of consent, communication, and respect within intimate relationships. This heightened awareness contributes to creating healthier, more consensual, and mutually respectful connections.

11. **Empowering Individuals:** Understanding the spiritual aspects of sexuality empowers individuals to make conscious and informed choices about their intimate lives. It encourages autonomy, self-expression, and a sense of empowerment in navigating one's sexual journey.

12. **Aligning with Personal Values**: For those with spiritual or religious beliefs, exploring the spiritual dimensions of sex allows for a deeper alignment between one's intimate life and personal values. It provides a framework for living in accordance with one's spiritual principles and the freedom to enjoy spiritual intimacy.

13. **Healing and Transformation:** In cases where individuals have experienced sexual trauma or challenges, the spiritual exploration of sex can be a path to healing and transformation. It offers a holistic perspective that goes beyond physical healing, encompassing emotional and spiritual recovery.

14. **Contributing to Wholeness:** Integrating spirituality into sexuality contributes to a sense of wholeness and completeness within individuals. It acknowledges and embraces the multifaceted nature of human beings, recognizing the importance of nurturing both the spiritual and physical aspects of self.

15. **Creating Sacred Moments:** By recognizing the sacred dimensions of sex, individuals can consciously create moments of sacredness within their intimate relationships. This intentional approach elevates the significance of these connections, making them more meaningful and fulfilling.

16. **Navigating Life Transitions**: Exploring the spiritual dimensions of sex becomes especially relevant during various life transitions, such as marriage, parenthood, or aging. It offers a framework for navigating these transitions with mindfulness, understanding, and a sense of the sacred.

In principle, the significance of exploring the spiritual dimensions of sex extends far beyond individual experiences. It contributes to societal shifts, cultural evolution, and the ongoing quest for a more holistic and enlightened approach to human sexuality. Exploring the spiritual dimensions of sex is a transformative and empowering journey that can positively impact individuals, relationships, and the broader cultural understanding of sexuality. It invites a deeper connection with the sacred, fostering personal and collective well-being.

C. Viewing Sex Beyond the Physical Aspect.

Indeed, the understanding of sex extends far beyond a mere physical connection. Here are several dimensions that highlight the complexity and depth of the human sexual experience:

1. **Emotional Connection**: - Sex involves an intense emotional connection between individuals. It provides a unique platform for expressing love, vulnerability, and intimacy, fostering a deep bond that goes beyond the physical act.

2. Spiritual Connection: - For most, sex is a spiritual experience that transcends the physical realm. It can be seen as a sacred union, a moment of spiritual connection, and an opportunity for shared transcendence.

3. **Psychological Impact:** - Sex has significant psychological implications. It can influence emotions, mood, and mental well-being. Positive sexual experiences contribute to emotional satisfaction and overall mental health.

4. **Communication and Trust:** - Engaging in sexual activity requires effective communication and trust between partners. It involves expressing desires, boundaries, and consent, fostering a healthy and respectful relationship.

5. **Expression of Identity**: - Sexuality is a fundamental aspect of human identity. It plays a role in self-discovery, self-expression, and the exploration of one's desires, contributing to a holistic understanding of oneself.

6. **Cultural and Social Context:** - Sex is embedded in cultural and social contexts, influencing societal norms, expectations, and behaviors. It serves as a means of connecting with cultural values, traditions, and evolving social dynamics.

7. **Procreation and Family Bond:** - Sex is intricately linked to procreation and the continuation of the human species. It forms the basis of family bonds, providing a biological foundation for the creation and nurturing of new life.

8. **Health and Well-being:-** Positive sexual experiences contribute to physical health and overall well-being. It can reduce stress, improve cardiovascular health, and release endorphins, promoting a sense of happiness and fulfillment.

9. **Exploration and Intimacy:** - Sexuality involves the exploration of desires, preferences, and intimate connections. It allows individuals to share vulnerabilities, creating a space for mutual understanding and personal growth.

10. **Consent and Respect:** - Central to healthy sexual experiences is the concept of consent and mutual respect. Respecting boundaries and ensuring consensual engagement is essential for fostering positive and meaningful connections.

Understanding sex as a multifaceted experience encompassing emotional, spiritual, psychological, and social dimensions is crucial for cultivating healthy relationships and promoting overall well-being. It reflects the intricate interplay of physical and non-physical elements that contribute to the richness of the human sexual experience.

D. The Connection Between Sex and the Soul.

The connection between sex and the soul is a profound and complex aspect of human existence, often explored through spiritual, philosophical, and cultural lenses. Here are several perspectives on the relationship between sex and the soul:

1. **Sex as a Sacred Union:** - Many spiritual traditions view sex as a sacred union that extends beyond the physical realm. It is seen as a way for two souls to connect intimately, fostering a deeper understanding and shared spiritual experience.

2. **Spiritual Transcendence:** - Some spiritual teachings emphasize the potential for spiritual transcendence through sex. When approached with mindfulness and a focus on connection, sexual intimacy is believed to elevate the soul and contribute to personal and mutual spiritual growth.

3. **Kundalini Energy:** - In Eastern spiritual a practice, such as yoga and Tantra, there is a concept known as Kundalini energy. It is often associated with sexual energy and the idea that, through conscious practices, this energy can be awakened, leading to spiritual awakening and enlightenment.

4. **Emotional and Energetic Connection:** - Sex is considered a powerful means of establishing emotional and energetic connections between individuals. Beyond the physical act, it is believed that souls intertwine; creating a bond that transcends time and space.

5. **Expression of Divine Love:** - In some spiritual philosophies, sexual intimacy is seen as an expression of divine love. The act of giving

and receiving love in such a vulnerable and intimate manner is regarded as a reflection of the divine love that connects all beings.

6. **Healing and Wholeness:-** Sexuality is sometimes associated with the healing of the soul. The idea is that through authentic and consensual sexual experiences, individuals can experience a sense of wholeness, emotional healing, and a deeper connection with their authentic selves.

7. **Intimacy and Spiritual Connection:** - Sex is viewed as a vehicle for achieving deep intimacy and spiritual connection with a partner. This connection involves not just the physical bodies but a meeting of souls, contributing to a sense of unity and oneness.

8. **Balance and Harmony:** - Finding a balance between physical desires and spiritual aspirations is often emphasized. Maintaining harmony between the physical and spiritual aspects of one's being is seen as essential for overall well-being and soulful fulfillment.

9. **Transformation and Growth:** - Engaging in conscious and mindful sexual experiences is believed to contribute to personal transformation and soulful growth. It is seen as an opportunity for self-discovery and a catalyst for evolving on a spiritual level.

10. **Respect for the Sacred:** - Many spiritual teachings stress the importance of approaching sex with reverence and respect for its sacred nature. Viewing one's body, one's partner, and the act itself as sacred is integral to fostering a soulful connection.

The relationship between sex and the soul is multifaceted, encompassing the spiritual, emotional, and physical dimensions of human existence. The way individuals perceive and experience this connection often aligns with their spiritual beliefs, cultural background, and personal philosophies.

D. The Higher Purpose of Sex beyond the Physical Act.

The higher purpose of sex is a topic that has been explored through various logical, spiritual, and cultural lenses. While viewpoints and opinions may differ, several common themes always emerge when considering the potential higher purposes of sex:

1. **Sacred Union and Connection:** - Many spiritual traditions view the higher purpose of sex as a sacred union between individuals. It is seen as a means of connecting on a deep, spiritual level, fostering intimacy, and recognizing the divine within each other.

2. **Creation and Procreation:** - From a biological and spiritual standpoint, sex is intricately connected to the creation of new life. The act of procreation is often seen as a sacred responsibility, contributing to the perpetuation of the human species.

3. **Spiritual Growth and Transformation:** - Some spiritual teachings suggest that sex, when approached with consciousness and intentionality can be a catalyst for spiritual growth and personal transformation. It becomes a path for individuals to explore and understand themselves more deeply. Similarly, sex can be seen as an avenue for understanding the human spirit and soul at a deeper level.

4. **Expressing Love and Unity**: - Sex is regarded by many as a powerful expression of love and unity between partners. It goes beyond physical pleasure to become a profound way of connecting emotionally, spiritually, and energetically.

5. **Balancing Energies:** - In certain spiritual practices, sex is seen as a way to balance and harmonize energies within the body. It involves

the exchange of energies between partners, contributing to overall well-being and spiritual alignment.

6. **Honoring the Divine Feminine and Masculine:** - Some spiritual philosophies accentuate the importance of honoring the divine feminine and masculine energies within individuals. When approached consciously through mutual consent, sex is viewed as a sacred dance that brings these energies into balance and alignment.

7. **Gateway to Transcendence**: - In specific mystic traditions, sex is considered a gateway to transcendence and spiritual enlightenment. It is believed that, through the union of opposites, individuals can experience a deeper connection with the Divine.

8. **Cultivating Intimacy and Communication:** - Sex serves as a medium for cultivating intimacy and communication between partners. It involves a vulnerable exchange that fosters emotional connection and understanding.

9. **Healing and Wholeness:** - Sexuality is sometimes associated with healing and achieving a sense of wholeness. Engaging in consensual and respectful sexual experiences is believed to contribute to emotional well-being and spiritual healing.

10. **Mindful Presence and Awareness:** - Approaching sex with mindfulness and awareness is seen as a higher purpose. It involves being fully present in the moment, being fully aware (both physically and emotionally), appreciating the sacredness of the experience, and recognizing the divine within oneself and one's partner.

Ultimately, the higher purpose of sex is idiosyncratic and can vary based on each individual beliefs, cultural contexts, and spiritual perspectives. It often involves a holistic understanding that encompasses physical, emotional, and spiritual dimensions, fostering a sense of connection, love, and transcendence.

E. Spiritual Intimacy.

Spiritual intimacy refers to a deep, soulful connection between individuals that goes beyond the physical and emotional realms, encompassing the spiritual dimension of human existence. Here are key aspects of spiritual intimacy:

1. **Shared Values and Beliefs:** - Spiritual intimacy often involves a shared set of values, beliefs, or a common spiritual path. Couples who align spiritually find a profound connection in their shared worldview and understanding of the Divine.

2. **Sacred Communication**: - Engaging in open, honest, and sacred communication is a cornerstone of spiritual intimacy. Partners feel comfortable discussing their spiritual journeys, beliefs, and experiences without judgment.

3. **Mindful Presence:** - Being present with each other in a mindful and spiritual way is integral to spiritual intimacy. This involves deep listening, being fully engaged in the present moment, and appreciating the sacredness of each other's presence.

4. **Prayer and Meditation Together:** - Couples practicing spiritual intimacy often engage in joint spiritual practices, such as prayer or meditation. These shared moments of quiet reflection contribute to a sense of spiritual connection and unity.

5. **Supporting Spiritual Growth:** - Partners in spiritually intimate relationships actively support each other's spiritual growth and personal development. They encourage exploration, provide emotional support, and celebrate milestones in their individual spiritual journeys.

6. **Transcendent Experiences:** - Spiritual intimacy can involve transcendent experiences where couples feel a deep, almost preternatural connection that goes beyond the physical and emotional realms. These moments are often considered sacred and profound.

7. **Symbolic Rituals:** - Engaging in symbolic rituals or ceremonies can enhance spiritual intimacy. This might include rituals for special occasions, shared prayer times, or other practices that symbolize their spiritual connection.

8. **Respect for Individual Paths**: - Respecting and honoring each other's individual spiritual paths is crucial. Spiritual intimacy doesn't necessarily require complete alignment in beliefs but involves an appreciation for the uniqueness of each partner's journey.

9. **Shared Service or Purpose:** - Some spiritually intimate couples find connection in shared service or a common purpose that aligns with their spiritual values. This could involve volunteering, contributing to a cause, or engaging in activities that promote positive change.

10. **Expressing Gratitude:** - Gratitude for the spiritual connection and the Divine presence in each other's lives is a common aspect of spiritual intimacy. Expressing gratitude fosters a sense of appreciation and deepens the spiritual bond.

Spiritual intimacy involves a shared exploration of the sacred within and around the couple. It goes beyond the surface and dives into the profound, creating a connection that nurtures the spiritual growth and well-being of both individuals in the relationship.

F. The interconnectedness of Sexuality and Spirituality.

The interconnectedness of sexuality and spirituality reflects the weighty integration of two vital aspects of human existence. Here are key facets that highlight their intricate relationship:

1. **Sacred Union:** - Many spiritual traditions emphasize the sacred nature of sexual union. Sex is seen as a sacred act that brings individuals into a deep, spiritual connection, mirroring the unity of opposites and expressing divine qualities.

2. **Spiritual Growth through Sexuality:** - Some spiritual teachings suggest that engaging in conscious and mindful sexual experiences can contribute to spiritual growth. The act of intimacy, when approached with intentionality and awareness, becomes a path for personal and mutual positive transformation.

3. **Energetic Exchange:** - Sex is associated with the exchange of energy between partners. From a spiritual perspective, this energetic connection can be seen as a merging of spiritual essences, creating a shared and powerful energy field.

4. **Tantric and Yogic Practices**: - Traditions like Tantra and certain yogic practices recognize the integration of sexuality and spirituality. These practices often involve the conscious channeling of sexual energy for spiritual awakening, emphasizing the interplay between the physical and spiritual dimensions for furtherance of a deeper spiritual experience.

5. **Chakras and Energetic Centers:** - In some spiritual philosophies, the body's energy centers, known as chakras, are linked

to sexuality. Practices aim to balance and align these energy centers, acknowledging the spiritual significance of sexual energy within the human experience. This sacred union should be engaged with total consciousness for the sanctity it upholds.

6. **Expressing Love and Connection:** - Sexuality is considered as a powerful means of expressing love, intimacy, honor, and connection. The act of physically uniting as one is seen as a reflection of the spiritual connection shared between partners. Partners need to honor this union for the sake of their emotional, physical and mental well-being.

7. **Transcendence through Intimacy:** - Moments of sexual intimacy are time and again considered opportunities for transcending the ordinary and experiencing a connection that goes beyond the physical. This transcendence can lead to a sense of oneness with the Divine.

8. **Creation and Divine Essence:** - The act of procreation is seen as a divine process in many spiritual traditions. Sexuality is linked to the creative force of the universe, highlighting the sacredness of bringing life into the world.

9. **Mindful Presence:** - Mindfulness plays a fundamental role in the interconnectedness of sexuality and spirituality. Being fully present during intimate moments fosters a deeper connection with one's partner and a heightened awareness of the spiritual dimensions within the experience.

10. **Holistic Well-being:** - Recognizing the integration of physical, emotional, and spiritual well-being, the interconnectedness of sexuality and spirituality promotes a holistic approach to human experience. It encourages individuals to honor and nurture all aspects of their being. To take keen effort in safeguarding the mystic interconnectedness that sex offers.

Understanding and embracing the interconnectedness of sexuality and spirituality can lead to a more profound, meaningful, and conscious experience of intimacy. It invites individuals to explore the depths of their spiritual selves within the context of their sexual relationships.

G. The Conscious and Unconscious Aspects of Sex..

Sex harbors both conscious and unconscious connections, reflecting the intricate interplay between the physical, emotional, and psychological dimensions of human experience. Here are insights into both the conscious and unconscious aspects of the connections associated with sex:

A. Conscious Connections:

1. **Physical Pleasure:** - On a conscious level, sex is often associated with physical pleasure and satisfaction. It involves the awareness of sensory experiences, arousal, and the fulfillment of fleshly desires.

2. **Emotional Intimacy:** - Conscious connections in sex extend to emotional intimacy. Individuals consciously seek and foster emotional bonds with their partners, recognizing the importance of shared feelings, trust, and vulnerability.

3. **Communication and Consent**: - Conscious connections involve clear communication and mutual consent. Partners are actively aware of each other's boundaries, desires, and preferences, fostering a respectful and consensual sexual experience.

4. **Articulating Love and Affection:** - Sex is a conscious manifestation of love and affection between partners. It involves a deliberate choice to connect on a deeper level emotionally and physically, fostering a sense of closeness and connection.

5. Shared Spiritual Practices: - For some individuals, conscious connections during sex include shared spiritual practices, such as meditation or prayer. Couples intentionally integrate spiritual dimensions into their sexual experiences, fostering a deeper connection on a conscious level.

A. Unconscious Connections:

1. Deep-seated Desires and Fears: - Unconscious connections in sex often stem from deep-seated desires and fears. Individuals may be driven by subconscious motivations rooted in past experiences or societal influences, impacting their sexual behaviors, both in positivity and often in negativity.

2. Symbolism and Imagery: - Sex can carry unconscious symbolism and imagery. Certain acts or preferences may have symbolic meanings that individuals might not consciously recognize but are influenced by on a subconscious level.

3. Repetition of Patterns: - Unconscious connections may involve the repetition of relational or sexual patterns. Individuals may unknowingly recreate dynamics from past relationships or family experiences, influencing their current sexual interactions.

4. Body Image and Self-esteem: - Unconscious connections with sex can be influenced by body image and self-esteem issues. These factors may impact how individuals perceive themselves and engage in sexual relationships without them being fully aware of the underlying dynamics.

5. Cultural and Social Conditioning: - Unconscious connections often result from cultural and social conditioning. Societal norms and expectations around sex can unconsciously shape individuals' beliefs, attitudes, and behaviors in the realm of sexuality.

Understanding both the conscious and unconscious connections associated with sex allows individuals to navigate their experiences more consciously. It invites self-reflection, communication with partners, and a deeper exploration of the complex interplay between conscious intentions and unconscious influences in the realm of human sexuality.

II. CHAPTER 1: UNVEILING THE SACRED CONNECTION

"Unveiling the Sacred Connection" invites individuals to embark on a profound exploration of the spiritual dimensions intertwined with human sexuality. This introductory chapter sets the stage for a transformative journey, urging readers to lift the veil that often shrouds the sacred nature of intimate connections.

1. **Understanding the Spiritual Essence:** The chapter delves into the essence of the spiritual in sexuality, encouraging readers to perceive beyond the physical and embrace the spiritual underpinnings of human intimacy. It lays the groundwork for a deeper grasp of the interconnectedness between the spiritual and the sensual.

2. **The Sacred Union in Various Traditions:** Drawing inspiration from diverse spiritual traditions, this segment explores how different cultures have revered and celebrated the sacred union in sexuality. It sheds light on the universal themes that connect these traditions, emphasizing the timeless nature of the spiritual aspects of sex.

3. **Embracing the Positive Potential:** Unveiling the sacred connection emphasizes the positive potential embedded in spiritual intimacy. It calls attention to the transformative power of sacred connections, offering a glimpse into the profound personal and relational growth that can unfold when individuals embrace the spiritual dimensions of their sexuality.

This opening chapter sets the tone for the book, encouraging readers and critics at large to approach the exploration with an open heart and a curious mind. It acts as a guiding light, inviting individuals to recognize and honor the sacred threads woven within the fabric of human connection, via their sexual appetites sparking a sense of awe for the transformative potential of the intimate and the Divine.

A. Understanding the Spiritual Essence of Sex

Understanding the spiritual essence of sex delves into the profound and sacred aspects that transcend the physical act. This exploration goes beyond societal norms and conventions, inviting individuals to contemplate the deeper layers of intimacy and connection. The essence of this understanding includes:

1. **Holistic View of Human Existence:** Recognizing that humans are multidimensional beings with physical, emotional, and spiritual aspects. Understanding the spiritual essence of sex involves acknowledging and integrating these dimensions, fostering a sense of completeness.

2. **Sacred Energy Exchange:** Viewing sex as more than a biological function, this understanding sees it as an exchange of sacred energy. The physical union becomes a conduit for emotional and spiritual energies, creating a shared experience that extends beyond the material realm.

3. **Connection with the Divine:** Acknowledging that intimate connections can be a pathway to connecting with the Divine or a higher source. This perspective considers sexuality as a sacred expression of the life force or universal energy, emphasizing the spiritual significance of such connections.

4. **Transcendence of Ego:** Understanding the spiritual essence of sex involves transcending the ego and societal conditioning. It encourages individuals to approach intimacy with authenticity,

vulnerability, and a deep sense of connection, moving beyond external expectations and judgments.

5. **Mindful Presence:** Emphasizing the importance of mindful presence during intimate moments, this understanding encourages individuals to be fully present in body, mind, and spirit. It involves letting go of distractions and cultivating a heightened awareness of the sacredness unfolding in the present moment.

6. **Spiritual Growth and Evolution**: Viewing sex as a catalyst for spiritual growth and evolution. This perspective sees intimate connections as opportunities for personal and relational development, fostering qualities such as compassion, understanding, and unconditional love.

7. **Alignment with Higher Values:** Understanding the spiritual essence of sex involves aligning intimate connections with higher values and principles. This may include integrity, respect, and a commitment to mutual well-being, ensuring that the spiritual aspects of sex are in harmony with one's ethical and moral framework.

8. **Honoring the Sacred Temple:** Recognizing the body as a sacred temple, this understanding encourages individuals to approach their own bodies and the bodies of their partners with veneration. It involves cultivating a positive and appreciative relationship with one's own physical form, understanding its role as a vessel for spiritual expression as well as deeper connections.

9. **Union of Hearts and Souls:** Understanding the spiritual essence of sex involves perceiving it as a union not only of bodies but also of hearts and souls. It acknowledges the potential for deeper emotional and spiritual bonding that go beyond the physical realm, creating a profound sense of oneness.

10. **Integration of Pleasure and Spirituality:** Dispelling the notion that pleasure and spirituality are mutually exclusive, this perspective sees pleasure as a natural and divine aspect of intimate connections. It encourages individuals to embrace pleasure with a sense

of gratitude and mindfulness, recognizing it as a gift within the spiritual journey.

11. **Symbolism of Creation and Manifestation:** Viewing sexual union as a symbolic act of creation and manifestation. This understanding aligns with the idea that the energy exchanged during intimate moments holds the potential for creative expression and the manifestation of shared intentions, whether on a personal or relational level.

12. **Harmony with Natural Rhythms:** Recognizing the importance of aligning intimate connections with natural rhythms, cycles, and seasons. This perspective embraces the cyclical nature of life, honoring the ebb and flow within relationships and understanding that each phase contributes to the overall spiritual growth.

13. **Sacred Ritual and Ceremony:** Incorporating the concept of sacred ritual and ceremony into intimate connections. This involves intentional practices, prayers, or symbolic gestures that elevate the spiritual significance of the moment, transforming ordinary acts into sacred expressions of love and unity.

14. **Expression of Unconditional Love**: Understanding the spiritual essence of sex emphasizes the expression of unconditional love. It sees intimate connections as an opportunity to express love without judgment, conditions, or expectations, fostering an atmosphere of acceptance and deep connection.

15. **Transcending Dualities:** Moving beyond dualities such as sacred versus profane or spiritual versus physical. This understanding encourages a holistic view where all aspects of human experience, including sexuality, are recognized as integral components of the spiritual journey.

The spiritual essence of sex encompasses a holistic, inclusive, and transformative perspective that transcends societal norms and limitations. It invites individuals to embark on a sacred exploration of their own intimate connections, fostering personal and relational growth within the rich tapestry of the spiritual journey. It encourages a shift in perception, recognizing the sacred nature of the connection between individuals, fostering a sense of reverence, and inviting a transformative journey within the realm of sexuality.

B. The Sacred Union in Various Spiritual Traditions

The concept of the sacred union holds profound significance in various spiritual traditions around the world, reflecting diverse perspectives on the intertwining of spirituality and sexuality. Here are glimpses into how different traditions perceive and celebrate the sacred union:

1. **Tantra in Hinduism:** - Hindu Tantra views the sacred union, often referred to as Maithuna, as a divine act that symbolizes the union of Shiva and Shakti, representing the cosmic forces of masculine and feminine energies. It is considered a path to spiritual enlightenment and an exploration of the divine within the human experience. (**Maithuna** is a Sanskrit term for sexual intercourse within Tantra, or alternatively for the sexual fluids generated or the couple participating in the ritual. It is the most important of the Panchamakara and constitutes the main part of the grand ritual of Tantra also known as Tattva Chakra. Wikipedia[1])

2. **Kabbalah in Judaism:** - In Kabbalistic teachings, the sacred union is associated with the unification of the divine masculine and feminine principles. The Song of Songs in the Hebrew Bible is interpreted allegorically, symbolizing the passionate and mystical relationship between God and the soul.

3. **Christian Mysticism:** - Christian mystics have explored the idea of the sacred union as the soul's union with God. *The writings of mystics like St. John of the Cross and St. Teresa of Avila* use romantic metaphors to describe the soul's intimate journey towards union with the divine.

---

1.   https://en.wikipedia.org/wiki/Maithuna

4. **Sufism in Islam:** - Sufi poetry often employs the metaphor of the lover and the beloved to describe the seeker's longing for union with the divine. The sacred union, in this context, represents the profound connection between the individual soul (the lover) and Allah (the beloved).

5. **Taoism:** - Taoist philosophy, especially in the context of sexual practices, emphasizes the harmonious union of Yin and Yang energies. The sacred union is seen as an expression of balance and harmony within the individual and the cosmos, aligning with the natural flow of energies.

6. **Native American Spirituality:** - In some Native American traditions, ceremonies and rituals associated with sacred union symbolize the interconnectedness of individuals with nature and the spiritual realm. These rituals often involve a deep reverence for the Earth and a celebration of life's cyclical nature.

7. **Ancient Egyptian Mysticism:** - In ancient Egyptian spirituality, the sacred union was symbolized through the union of Osiris and Isis. This symbolic representation emphasized the cyclical nature of life, death, and rebirth, reflecting the eternal and transformative aspects of the divine union.

8. **Buddhism:** - While Buddhism tends to approach sexuality with a focus on ethical conduct and mindfulness, certain Buddhist Tantric practices explore the sacred dimensions of union. These practices aim at transcending dualities and realizing the interconnectedness of all things.

9. **Ancient Greek Mysteries:** - In the Eleusinian Mysteries of ancient Greece, the sacred union was symbolized through the myth of Demeter and Persephone. The cycle of Persephone's descent into the underworld and return represents the eternal rhythms of nature, fertility, and the cyclical nature of life and death.

10. **Shamanic Practices:** - In various indigenous shamanic traditions, the sacred union is often expressed through rituals that

involve the union of opposites, representing the interconnectedness of all things. These ceremonies may incorporate dance, music, and symbolic acts to evoke spiritual experiences.

11. **Chinese Taoist Alchemy:** - Taoist alchemy delves into the concept of the sacred union through inner alchemical practices. The harmonization of Yin and Yang within the body is seen as a path to spiritual enlightenment, where the individual aligns with the cosmic forces to attain balance and vitality.

12. **Ancient Mayan Spirituality:** - Mayan civilization had rituals and ceremonies that celebrated the sacred union, often tied to agricultural cycles and the worship of fertility deities. These practices were symbolic of the interconnectedness between human life, the cycles of nature, and the divine.

13. **Jainism:** - Jain teachings emphasize the importance of practicing celibacy for spiritual progress. However, for those on the household path, the concept of the sacred union is acknowledged within the bounds of dharma (righteous living), emphasizing mutual respect, love, and responsibility.

14. **African Traditional Religions:** - Various African traditional religions incorporate sacred ceremonies that honor the sacred union, recognizing the divine aspects within human relationships. Rituals often involve dance, music, and symbolic gestures to invoke spiritual blessings and harmony.

15. **Mesoamerican Cultures:** - The Aztecs and other Mesoamerican cultures had rituals that celebrated the sacred union, often associated with agricultural fertility. These ceremonies incorporated dance, music, and offerings to invoke the divine forces for prosperity and abundance.

16. **Shinto in Japan:** - Shinto, the indigenous spirituality of Japan, recognizes the sacredness of union in rituals and festivals. Ceremonies may involve prayers for fertility, prosperity, and harmonious

relationships, reflecting the interconnectedness of the spiritual and natural worlds.

In each of these traditions, the sacred union serves as a symbolic and transformative expression, weaving threads of spirituality into the fabric of human experience. Whether through myths, rituals, or philosophical teachings, the concept underscores the profound and universal nature of the spiritual dimensions within intimate connections.

Across these traditions, the sacred union is a recurring theme, emphasizing the interconnectedness of the physical and spiritual realms, the balance of energies, and the transformative potential of intimate connections on the path toward spiritual realization.

C. Embracing the Positive Potential

"Embracing the Positive Potential" is an invitation to explore the transformative and uplifting aspects of recognizing the spiritual dimensions within intimate connections. This section unfolds as a celebration of the profound positivity that can emerge when individuals consciously engage with the sacred essence of sex. Main themes include:

1. **Spiritual Intimacy and Connection:** - Delving into the positive potential of spiritual intimacy, this section highlights how recognizing the sacred within oneself and a partner fosters a deeper, more meaningful connection. It explores how shared spiritual experiences can enhance emotional bonds and create a sense of oneness. The Bible encourages the coming together of two people and them become one through their sacred union; *"For this reason, a man will leave his father and mother and be united to his wife, and the two will become one flesh." (Genesis 2:24)*

2. **Fostering Emotional and Energetic Bonds:** - This section emphasizes the positive impact of spiritual awareness on emotional and energetic bonds. It explores how a heightened sense of spirituality can contribute to emotional intelligence, empathy, and a shared energetic resonance between individuals engaged in a sacred union.

3. **Personal Growth and Transformation:** - Central to embracing the positive potential is the exploration of how spiritual dimensions within intimate connections serve as catalysts for personal growth and transformation. This section illustrates how such connections can

inspire self-discovery, resilience, and the evolution of individuals on their spiritual journeys.

4. **Cultivating Mindful and Sacred Sexuality**: - Mindfulness becomes a key theme as the chapter explores the positive potential of cultivating a heightened awareness during intimate moments. It discusses how incorporating sacred elements into sexuality leads to a more conscious and intentional approach, fostering a sense of reverence and appreciation. This also brings in the concept of honor for each other; *"Let marriage be held in honor among all, and let the marriage bed be undefiled..." (Hebrews 13:4)*

5. **Aligning with Higher Values:** - Emphasizing the alignment of intimate connections with higher values, this section explores how recognizing the sacred aspects of sex encourages individuals to approach relationships with integrity, respect, and a commitment to mutual well-being. It sheds light on the positive impact on ethical and moral frameworks. It portrays the sacrificial aspect that this sacred union calls for; the Bible states calls out this form of sacrifice and encourages it, - *"Husbands, love your wives, just as Christ loved the church and gave himself up for her." (Ephesians 5:25)*

6. **Harmonizing the Physical and Spiritual Realms:** - The chapter explores the harmonization of physical desires with spiritual principles, portraying the positive potential of integrating these realms. It delves into the idea that such alignment contributes to a balanced and holistic approach to human sexuality. In the Christian circles, the body is called the temple of the Holy Spirit and thus should be treated with reverence and honor; *"Or do you not know that your bodies are temples of the Holy Spirit, who is in you, whom you have received from God?" (1 Corinthians 6:19)*

7. **Sacred Moments of Connection:** - This section delves into the creation of sacred moments within intimate connections. Let that which has been joined through this sacred union not be set apart; *"So they are no longer two, but one flesh. Therefore, what God has joined*

*together, let no one separate." (**Matthew 19:6**).* Acknowledging the spiritual dimensions transforms ordinary moments into profound, sacred experiences. These moments become opportunities for individuals to connect with each other on a soulful level.

8. **Enhanced Sensuality and Pleasure:** - The chapter celebrates the positive potential of heightened sensuality and pleasure within the context of spiritual awareness. This awareness commands blessings and the possibility of much joy in the union; *"May your fountain be blessed, and may you rejoice in the wife of your youth." (**Proverbs 5:18**).* This suggests that an understanding of the sacred aspects of sex can amplify the sensory experience, fostering a deep appreciation for the physical and spiritual dimensions of pleasure.

9. **Emotional Fulfillment and Well-being**: - Embracing the positive potential involves recognizing the impact of spiritual dimensions on emotional fulfillment and overall well-being. This section explores how individuals who engage in sacred unions may experience increased emotional satisfaction, a greater sense of purpose, and improved mental health.

10. **Nurturing Unconditional Love:** - Unconditional love becomes a focal point as the chapter explores its positive potential within intimate connections. Understanding the sacred essence of sex encourages individuals to cultivate love that transcends conditions and judgments, fostering a profound and enduring connection.

11. **Transcending Cultural Stigmas:** - This section examines how the positive potential of embracing the sacred in sex extends to transcending cultural stigmas. By recognizing the spiritual dimensions, individuals may challenge societal norms, fostering acceptance and celebrating diverse expressions of intimacy.

12. **Empowering Individual and Collective Growth:** - The positive potential of spiritual intimacy is portrayed as an empowering force for individual and collective growth. It explores how these connections can inspire not only personal transformation but also

contribute to a broader cultural shift towards a more enlightened and accepting perspective on sexuality.

13. **Cultivating Gratitude and Reverence:** - Gratitude and reverence become integral aspects of embracing the positive potential. This section discusses how individuals engaged in sacred unions may develop a deep sense of gratitude for the beauty of intimate connections and a reverent acknowledgment of the divine within themselves and their partners.

14. **Elevating Shared Goals and Intentions:** - The chapter underscores how embracing the sacred dimensions within intimate connections can elevate shared goals and intentions. Partners aligned spiritually may find themselves working towards common aspirations, creating a synergistic effect that extends beyond the confines of the relationship.

In summary, "Embracing the Positive Potential" illuminates the myriad ways in which recognizing and celebrating the spiritual aspects of intimate connections can bring about positive transformations in individuals, relationships, and the broader cultural landscape. It becomes a testament to the beauty and richness that unfolds when the sacred is acknowledged within the realm of human sexuality.

It paints a vibrant picture of the beauty that unfolds when individuals consciously engage with the sacred dimensions of their intimate connections. And also serves as an affirmation of the enriching experiences, personal growth, and profound connections that can blossom when the positive potential within spiritual intimacy is recognized and celebrated.

III. CHAPTER 2: POSITIVE CONSEQUENCES

Positive Consequences unfolds as a celebration of the uplifting outcomes that arise from acknowledging and nurturing the spiritual dimensions within intimate connections. This chapter explores the profound positivity embedded in recognizing the sacred essence of sex. The chapter unfolds with a focus on the positive consequences of deep emotional and energetic connections. Key themes include:

1. **Spiritual Intimacy and Connection:** - Exploration of *Genesis 2:24* - *"For this reason, a man will leave his father and mother and be united to his wife, and the two will become one flesh."* This biblical verse is used to underscore the spiritual significance of becoming one in a sacred union. Acknowledging and nurturing spiritual dimensions within intimate connections create a shared spiritual journey for partners. By understanding the biblical concept of becoming "one flesh," couples are encouraged to embark on a joint exploration of spiritual growth, fostering a deep and interconnected bond.

Reflections on the biblical teaching of leaving one's father and mother highlight the idea of transcending societal and familial boundaries in the pursuit of spiritual intimacy. This encourages couples to forge a unique and sacred connection, free from external expectations, as they unite in a shared commitment to spiritual exploration.

Referencing the concept of becoming "one flesh" underscores the idea of oneness not only on a physical level but also in spirit. The chapter explores how recognizing the spiritual essence of the union deepens the connection, fostering a sense of unity that goes beyond the surface, creating a profound and lasting bond.

Drawing inspiration still, from the concept of becoming *"one flesh"* *(Genesis 2:24),* the chapter explores how spiritual intimacy enables communication beyond words. Couples are encouraged to cultivate a deep understanding and connection that transcends verbal expressions, allowing for a profound and intuitive communion of spirits.

2. **Fostering Emotional and Energetic Bonds**: - Reflection on *1 Peter 4:8* - *"Above all, love each other deeply because love covers over a multitude of sins."* This verse becomes a touchstone for discussing the transformative power of deep love in fostering emotional and energetic bonds. The chapter explores how spiritual intimacy enhances emotional depth. Couples are encouraged to navigate challenges with love, forgiveness, and empathy, fostering emotional resilience and strengthening the bond forged through shared spirituality.

The chapter emphasizes the creation of sacred bonds within intimate connections, echoing the biblical principle that *"what God has joined together, let no one separate"* *(Matthew 19:6)*. These bonds become opportunities for couples to experience a divine connection, reinforcing their commitment to a spiritual union that transcends temporal challenges.

Referencing the biblical principle of love covering sins, this chapter emphasizes the transformative power of forgiveness within intimate connections. Couples are guided to view forgiveness as a sacred act, promoting emotional healing and creating a resilient foundation for their relationship.

Building on the concept of energetic resonance, the chapter, additionally introduces the idea of cultivating energetic awareness. Couples are encouraged to pay attention to the subtle energies within their connection, fostering a heightened sensitivity to the emotional currents that contribute to their shared energetic bond.

3. **Personal Growth and Transformation:** Building on the biblical foundation, the chapter explores how recognizing and nurturing spiritual intimacy leads to mutual support in each other's spiritual journeys. Couples are encouraged to embark on individual spiritual journeys, aligning with the biblical concept of personal transformation. Recognizing that each partner is on a unique path of growth fosters mutual respect and an environment conducive to personal and spiritual development. Couples are encouraged to be companions in their pursuit of spiritual growth, creating an environment where both partners can flourish in their connection with the divine.

Couples are inspired by *2 Peter 3:18*, *"But grow in the grace and knowledge of our Lord and Savior Jesus Christ,"* to view personal evolution as a source of empowerment. The relationship becomes a space where partners can grow individually, contributing to the enrichment of the union.

Integration of *Romans 12:2 - "Do not conform to the pattern of this world, but be transformed by the renewing of your mind."* This biblical guidance is woven into the discussion on how recognizing spiritual dimensions leads to personal growth and transformation. To not look at how the world does it but to be open to learn new ways that benefits the couple's individuality. In line with this call for transformation and renewal in *Romans 12:2*, the chapter further explores how acknowledging spiritual dimensions allows couples to embrace vulnerability and authenticity. By creating a safe space for openness, partners can share their spiritual selves, fostering a deeper connection built on genuine understanding. Couples are also encouraged to transform together, creating a space where authenticity and openness become pillars of their emotional connection.

4. **Cultivating Mindful and Sacred Sexuality:** - Drawing inspiration from the sacredness of the marriage bed in *Hebrews 13:4 - "Let marriage be held in honor among all, and let the marriage bed*

be undefiled." The chapter encourages couples to cultivate a sense of reverence within their intimate moments. Recognizing the spiritual dimensions elevates physical intimacy to a sacred act, fostering a profound and respectful approach to the expression of love. This verse becomes a foundation for discussing the importance of maintaining sacredness within the marital relationship. Seeking out positive ways to remain faithful to your partner and fostering a sacred space to discuss potential pitfalls of the relationship.

5. **Aligning with Higher Spiritual Values:** - In reference to *Ephesians 5:25* - *"Husbands, love your wives, just as Christ loved the church and gave himself up for her."* This biblical teaching underlines the significance of aligning intimate connections with the sacrificial and selfless love exemplified by Christ. This often fosters a timeless relationship based on unconditional love that stems from the Divine and portrayed through loving actions. Reflecting further on the biblical teaching of husbands loving their wives as Christ loved the church **(Ephesians 5:25),** the chapter underscores how spiritual intimacy becomes the foundation for unconditional love. Couples are encouraged to emulate divine love, fostering a relationship where love is patient, kind, and enduring. Christ's sacrificial love emphasizes how couples can engage in shared spiritual practices. Whether through prayer, meditation, or joint participation in religious rituals, these practices deepen the spiritual connection, creating a shared sacred space within the relationship.

Drawing also from *Philippians 4:8*, *"Whatever is true, whatever is noble, whatever is right, whatever is pure, whatever is lovely, whatever is admirable—if anything is excellent or praiseworthy—think about such things,"* couples are guided to integrate spiritual practices into their personal growth journeys. This includes meditation, prayer, and reflection.

Building on the concept of aligning with spiritual values, couples are guided by *Philippians 3:14*, *"I press on toward the goal for the prize of the upward call of God in Christ Jesus."* They are encouraged to set and pursue spiritual goals individually and collectively, creating a shared vision that aligns with their faith.

6. **A Source of Comfort and Strength:** - Relationships often offer a source of comfort and strength; referencing passages that highlight the comfort and strength found in spiritual connections *(Psalm 34:18, Isaiah 41:10),* the chapter emphasizes how recognizing the sacred within intimate relationships becomes a source of solace during life's trials. Couples find reassurance in their shared faith and reliance on a higher power.

7. **Deep Empathy and Understanding**: - Building on the biblical wisdom, the positive consequences explores how acknowledging the sacred within intimate relationships fosters deep empathy and understanding. Couples are encouraged to embrace each other's vulnerabilities, creating a compassionate and supportive space where emotional nuances are honored. Creating a judgment free space for all manner of discussions builds an empathetic relationship based on mutual understanding and support.

In accepting each other couples are guided to cultivate compassion and empathy. This fosters an environment where partners not only understand each other's emotions but actively support and uplift one another in times of need.

8. **Shared Emotional Resilience:** - Drawing inspiration from *Ecclesiastes 4:9-10, "Two are better than one... If either of them falls down, one can help the other up,"* couples are guided to create a supportive environment for each other's personal growth. The relationship becomes a catalyst for positive transformation, offering encouragement and assistance.

Another positive consequence of sacred union is shared emotional resilience; reflecting on biblical teachings, couples are guided to build shared emotional resilience. This chapter emphasizes how recognizing the sacred essence within the relationship allows partners to weather life's storms together, finding strength in their connection and an unwavering commitment to one another.

This theme of resilience further explores the biblical principle of resilience in *Psalm 23:4, "Even though I walk through the darkest valley, I will fear no evil."* Couples are guided to cultivate resilience through personal growth, viewing challenges as opportunities for transformation and drawing strength from their spiritual foundation.

9. **Energetic Alignment:** - This positive concept of energetic alignment is introduced, emphasizing how recognizing the spiritual dimensions within intimate connections leads to an energetic resonance between partners. Couples are encouraged to cultivate a harmonious energy exchange, deepening their connection beyond the physical realm. Creating a spiritual sacred space though there naked connectedness brings about a sense of energetic alignment.

Building on the concept of energetic alignment, the chapter explores how couples can achieve harmony between the emotional and energetic realms. Recognizing that emotions carry energy, couples are encouraged to align their emotional states, fostering a balanced and resonant connection.

10. **Co-creation of Emotional Space:** - This positive consequence encourages couples to co-create an emotional space that reflects the sacred dimensions within their connection. This involves intentional efforts to foster emotional intimacy, share vulnerabilities, and engage in practices that deepen their emotional bond. This becomes a catalyst for supporting each other's emotional growth. Couples are guided to embrace personal evolution while remaining steadfast allies in their partner's journey.

11. **Elevating Emotional Intimacy Through Communication:** - The chapter emphasizes the importance of communication in fostering emotional intimacy. As a positive consequence couples are encouraged to engage in open and honest conversations, expressing their feelings

and thoughts. This communication becomes a sacred practice that deepens their emotional connection.

Communication becomes a transformative tool, aligning with **Colossians 4:6** *"Let your conversation be always full of grace."* Couples are encouraged to communicate with grace and kindness, fostering an environment where transformative conversations lead to mutual understanding and growth.

12. **Transcending Emotional Barriers:** - The concept of transcending emotional barriers is explored, encouraging couples to break down walls that may hinder emotional connection. By recognizing the sacredness within their relationship, partners can create a space where emotional barriers dissolve, allowing for a more profound and authentic bond. Couples are introduced to the idea of creating shared rituals that enhance emotional connection.

13. **Mindful Emotional Presence:** - Mindfulness as positive consequence in sacred union becomes a key theme as couples are guided to be fully present in their emotional exchanges. By incorporating mindfulness into their interactions, partners can deepen their emotional connection, savoring each moment with a heightened awareness of the sacredness within their relationship.

14. **Energetic Renewal through Love and Forgiveness:** - Couples are guided to renew their energetic connection through acts of love and forgiveness. Embracing forgiveness as a sacred practice allows partners to release stagnant energy, creating space for the rejuvenation of their emotional and energetic bonds.

15. **Expressing Gratitude for Emotional Connection:** - Gratitude becomes a central theme as couples are encouraged to express thankfulness for their emotional connection. Drawing inspiration from biblical teachings on gratitude, partners can acknowledge and celebrate the sacred gift of emotional intimacy within their relationship. Couples are guided by **1 Thessalonians 5:18**, *"Give thanks in all circumstances,"* to cultivate a gratitude practice in their

personal and shared experiences. Expressing gratitude becomes a transformative act that enhances perspective, resilience, and the overall sense of personal well-being.

16. **Balancing Independence and Togetherness**: - *Ecclesiastes 4:12, "A cord of three strands is not quickly broken,"* becomes a metaphor for balancing individual growth with togetherness. Couples are encouraged to weave their individual pursuits into the fabric of their relationship, creating a resilient bond that withstands the tests of personal evolution.

17. **Celebrating Milestones in Faith:** -This theme explores the idea of celebrating personal and spiritual milestones, drawing inspiration from *Psalm 118:24, "This is the day that the Lord has made; let us rejoice and be glad in it."* Couples are guided to commemorate significant moments in their individual spiritual journeys, fostering a sense of joy and gratitude.

18. **Navigating Challenges through Faith:** - Taking inspiration from *James 1:2-4, "Count it all joy, my brothers, when you meet trials of various kinds, for you know that the testing of your faith produces steadfastness,"* couples are guided to navigate challenges with faith. This theme explores how trials can become opportunities for personal and relational growth.

19. **Encouraging Lifelong Learning:** - Lifelong learning is a positive consequence that is encouraged, aligning with *Proverbs 18:15, "An intelligent heart acquires knowledge, and the ear of the wise seeks knowledge."* Couples are guided to view personal growth as a continual journey of acquiring wisdom, knowledge, and spiritual insights, fostering a shared commitment to lifelong learning.

20. **Creating a Legacy of Faith:** - Sacred union creates a faith legacy that goes beyond generations. As a positive consequence this theme concludes by exploring the idea of creating a legacy of faith, inspired by *Proverbs 22:6, "Train up a child in the way he should go; even when he is old he will not depart from it."* Couples are encouraged

to consider the impact of their personal growth on future generations, creating a legacy rooted in faith and transformation.

In entwining these aspects together, the chapter paints a comprehensive picture of spiritual intimacy and connection. It emphasizes that when couples embrace the positive consequences of recognizing the sacred within their relationships, they not only deepen their bond but also create a foundation for enduring love, support, and transformative growth.

The biblical references are seamlessly integrated to emphasize the positive consequences of embracing the spiritual dimensions within intimate connections. Each theme is explored through both biblical insights and practical considerations, creating a holistic understanding of the transformative and enriching outcomes that emerge from a sacred approach to sexuality. In essence, the exploration of spiritual intimacy and connection within the chapter seeks to elevate the understanding of intimacy to a sacred level. By interlacing biblical wisdom with practical insights, it encourages couples to embrace the positive consequences that arise when spiritual dimensions are acknowledged and celebrated within their intimate relationships.

In summary, this chapter unfolds as a guide for couples to embrace the positive consequences of recognizing and nurturing emotional and energetic bonds within their intimate relationships. By interlinking biblical insights with practical considerations, the chapter provides a roadmap for couples to deepen their connection on both emotional and energetic levels and also encourages couples to view personal evolution as a sacred and dynamic aspect of their shared journey.

IV. CHAPTER 3: NEGATIVE CONSEQUENCES

Chapter 3 delves into the intricate landscape of negative consequences within intimate connections when the sacred dimensions are overlooked. As relationships unfold in the intricate dance of shared existence, a lack of spiritual awareness can give rise to multifaceted challenges. Emotional strain, conflicts in life goals and resistance to personal growth emerge as potential pitfalls. The chapter delves into the impact on conflict resolution, struggles in intimacy, and the adoption of unhealthy coping mechanisms when the spiritual foundation is absent. Moreover, it explores the potential loss of purpose, strain on shared values, and challenges in parenting dynamics. Financial struggles, a decline in compassion, and repercussions on health and well-being are also scrutinized. The inability to navigate life transitions, and its effect on community and social connections, draws attention to the broader repercussions. Grounded in biblical wisdom, this chapter serves as a reflective exploration, urging couples to recognize the significance of spiritual nurturing in fostering resilience and fulfillment within their relationships.

Negative Consequences sheds light on the potential challenges and pitfalls that may arise when the sacred dimensions within intimate connections are overlooked or neglected. Grounded in the understanding that relationships are multifaceted, this chapter explores how the absence of spiritual awareness and nurturing can lead to adverse outcomes. Most of the negative consequences are:

1. **Spiritual Disconnect and Emotional Strain:** - Without a foundation in recognizing the sacred, couples may experience a spiritual disconnect. This can manifest as emotional strain, where the absence of shared spiritual values leads to misunderstandings, conflicts, and a sense of distance. This creates a further wedge between couple who have little awareness of the underlying spiritual rift.

2. **Lack of Alignment in Life Goals:** - Couples may face challenges when their life goals and aspirations lack alignment. The absence of shared spiritual values, inspired by *Proverbs 29:18* -*"Where there is no vision, the people perish"*, can result in a divergence of paths, causing friction and a sense of unfulfillment. Two people can no longer walk together unless they agree; *Amos 3:3*-*"Can two walk together, except they be agreed?"*

3. **Stagnation and Resistance to Growth:** - The chapter explores how a lack of spiritual awareness may contribute to stagnation in personal and relational growth. This negative consequence causes further friction by bringing the aspect of blame-game, the assumption that your partner has caused you to stagnate. Drawing from *2 Peter 3:18 ("But grow in the grace and knowledge of our Lord and Savior Jesus Christ");* it highlights the potential for resistance to transformative change when spiritual dimensions are overlooked.

4. **Conflict Resolution Challenges:** - The absence of spiritual grounding can pose challenges in conflict resolution. Couples may struggle to find common ground, in such scenarios, forgiveness is always elusive, and resolution may be hindered, reflecting the difficulties outlined in **Matthew 18:15-17** about resolving disputes within the community of believers.

5. **Intimacy Struggles**: - The chapter delves into how neglecting the spiritual dimensions can lead to struggles in physical and emotional intimacy. Referencing *1 Corinthians 7:5* -*"Do not deprive each other except perhaps by mutual consent and for a time, so that you may devote yourselves to prayer. Then come back together again so that Satan will not*

tempt you because of your lack of self-control", this Biblical verse explores how a lack of spiritual connection may impact the overall intimacy within the relationship.

6. **Unhealthy Coping Mechanisms:** - Couples may turn to unhealthy coping mechanisms in the absence of spiritual guidance. This will further break-down an already dying relationship. The chapter discusses how *Psalm 34:18 -"The Lord is near to the brokenhearted and saves the crushed in spirit"* underscores the importance of seeking guidance and solace in the Divine rather than resorting to detrimental coping strategies.

7. **Loss of Purpose and Meaning:** - The chapter also explores and brings to light the potential for a loss of purpose and meaning when spiritual dimensions are neglected. Inspired by *Ecclesiastes 12:13 ("Fear God and keep his commandments, for this is the duty of all mankind")*, it delves into how a lack of spiritual grounding may contribute to existential challenges within the relationship.

8. **Impact on Mental and Emotional Well-being**: - As a potentially negative consequence, neglecting the spiritual dimensions can impact mental and emotional well-being. As observed in the wisdom writings of the Bible, from *Proverbs 12:25- ("Anxiety weighs down the heart, but a kind word cheers it up")*, this chapter discusses how a lack of spiritual connection may contribute to heightened anxiety and emotional distress.

This chapter on the various negative consequences of a broken down spiritual sacred union serves as a reflection on the potential negative consequences that may emerge when the sacred aspects within intimate connections are disregarded. Its major aim is to raise awareness about the importance of spiritual nurturing in fostering a resilient and fulfilling relationship.

a.Distortions of Spiritual Energy

Diving deeper into the negative consequences of a distorted or an abominable sacred union is the theme of distortions of spiritual energy. This section of the book explores further the potential distortions that can occur in the realm of spiritual energy within intimate connections. Grounded in the understanding that spiritual energy is a dynamic force, the chapter discovers how various factors can lead to imbalances and distortions. Let's explore several key themes:

1. **Ego-driven Spiritual Imbalance:** - This theme examines the distortion caused by ego-driven motivations within spiritual energy. Referencing *Galatians 5:16* *("But I say, walk by the Spirit, and you will not gratify the desires of the flesh")*, this verse brings to light the essence of aligning spiritual energy with humility and selflessness, cautioning against ego-driven imbalances. Trying to satisfy the ego with heightened levels fleshly lust only break down an individual's mental health and well-being.

2. **Unresolved Emotional Baggage:** - Emotional baggage is a negative consequence that can be addressed simply by the couples willingness to forgive. Drawing inspiration from *Matthew 18:21-22* *("Lord, how many times shall I forgive my brother or sister who sins against me?")*, this section explores how unresolved emotional baggage can distort spiritual energy. Here a couple is encouraged to address and release lingering emotional wounds, fostering a more harmonious flow of spiritual energy.

3. **Misalignment of Intentions:** - The aspect of misalignment of intentions can create distortions in spiritual energy within

relationships. Referencing *Proverbs 16:3* *("Commit to the Lord whatever you do, and he will establish your plans"),* emphasizes the impact of aligning intentions with higher spiritual values to avoid discordant energy patterns.

4. Lack of Mindful Presence: - Sex as a form of sacred union should never be performed mindlessly. Mindfulness becomes a focal point; this section discusses how a lack of mindful presence can contribute to distortions in spiritual energy. **Psalm 46:10** calls for stillness and an acknowledgement of the Divine within the sacred union *("Be still, and know that I am God").* This verse puts ephasis**ss** couples to cultivate a mindful presence to enhance the clarity and purity of their spiritual energy exchanges.

5. **Inauthentic Expressions of Spirituality:** - With a view on *Matthew 23:27* *("Woe to you, teachers of the law and Pharisees, you hypocrites! You are like whitewashed tombs, which look beautiful on the outside but on the inside are full of the bones of the dead"),* this chapter explores the distortions that can arise from inauthentic expressions of spirituality. It advocates for genuine and heartfelt spiritual practices to maintain a sincere flow of energy.

6. **Neglect of Spiritual Practices**: - This section discusses how neglecting spiritual practices can contribute to imbalances in spiritual energy. As stated in *Colossians 3:16* *("Let the word of Christ dwell in you richly"),* it underscores the importance of regular spiritual practices to maintain a vibrant and nourishing flow of spiritual energy within the relationship.

7. **External Influences and Distractions:** - External influences and distractions are explored as potential disruptors of spiritual energy. Referencing *1 Corinthians 15:33* *("Do not be misled: 'Bad company corrupts good character'"),* here the emphasis is on the need to guard against influences that may lead to distortions in the sacred energy shared between partners.

This section sheds light on the intricacies of spiritual energy within intimate connections and how various factors can contribute to distortions. By drawing on biblical principles and practical insights, it guides couples towards cultivating a more balanced and authentic spiritual energy exchange within their relationship.

b.Impact on Mental and Emotional Well-being

This section explores how distortions in spiritual energy within intimate connections can have profound repercussions on the mental and emotional well-being of individuals and the relationship as a whole.

1. **Increased Stress and Anxiety:** - Distortions in spiritual energy may contribute to heightened stress and anxiety. Note the role of balanced spiritual energy in fostering peace and alleviating the burdens that contribute to stress and anxiety.

2. **Emotional Exhaustion:** - Distorted spiritual energy can lead to emotional exhaustion. Inspired by *Isaiah 40:31* *("But those who hope in the Lord will renew their strength")*, it highlights the importance of spiritual alignment for renewing emotional strength and preventing the draining effects of exhaustion.

3. **Strained Relationships and Communication:** - Distortions in spiritual energy may strain relationships and hinder effective communication. *Ephesians 4:29* states *("Do not let any unwholesome talk come out of your mouths, but only what is helpful for building others up")*, the section underscores how balanced spiritual energy contributes to harmonious communication and strengthened connections.

4. **Diminished Emotional Resilience:** - Distorted spiritual energy can diminish emotional resilience. Drawing from *Psalm 34:17-18* *("The righteous cry out, and the Lord hears them; he delivers them from all their troubles")*, it encourages individuals to seek spiritual alignment for enhanced emotional resilience in the face of life's challenges.

5. **Negative Impact on Self-esteem:** -Distortions in spiritual energy may negatively impact self-esteem. But taking a look at ***Psalm 139:14***, which states *("I praise you because I am fearfully and wonderfully made"),* this section emphasizes the role of balanced spiritual energy in fostering a positive self-image and preventing the erosion of self-esteem.

6. **Feelings of Isolation and Loneliness:** - Distorted spiritual energy can contribute to feelings of isolation and loneliness. Inspired by ***Psalm 68:6*** *("God sets the lonely in families"),* this verse encourages individuals to seek spiritual alignment to alleviate the sense of isolation and foster a deeper connection with others.

7. **Impact on Mental Clarity and Focus:** - Distorted spiritual energy may impact mental clarity and focus. From *1 Corinthians 14:33* which states *("For God is not a God of disorder but of peace"),* this section highlights how spiritual alignment contributes to a sense of peace and clarity, positively influencing mental well-being.

8. **Challenges in Coping with Life Transitions:** - Distortions in spiritual energy often pose challenges in coping with life transitions. Referencing ***Jeremiah 29:11*** *("For I know the plans I have for you"),* it encourages individuals to seek spiritual grounding to navigate transitions with a sense of purpose and assurance.

This section gives emphasis to the intricate connection between spiritual energy and mental/emotional well-being. It advocates for the cultivation of balanced and authentic spiritual energy within intimate connections as a cornerstone for maintaining mental and emotional health in individuals and relationships.

C. Strains on Spiritual Growth and Harmony

This section of the book delves into the various strains that can impact spiritual growth and harmony within intimate sacred connections, exploring the challenges that may hinder the shared journey of individuals seeking spiritual alignment.

1. **Divergent Spiritual Paths:** - Couples may face strains when their spiritual paths diverge. Drawing from *Amos 3:3 ("Can two walk together, unless they are agreed?"),* the section emphasizes the challenges of maintaining spiritual harmony when individuals follow separate spiritual trajectories.

2. **Mismatched Spiritual Priorities:** - Strains on spiritual growth and harmony arise from mismatched spiritual priorities within sacred relationships. *Matthew 6:33* calls for a higher priority; *("But seek first the kingdom of God and his righteousness"),* this verse highlights the importance of shared spiritual priorities to foster growth and harmony.

3. **Resistance to Personal Growth:** - Couples may experience strains when there is resistance to personal growth. Inspired by *Philippians 3:12 ("Not that I have already obtained all this, or have already arrived at my goal"),* the section encourages individuals to embrace personal growth as an essential component of the shared spiritual journey.

4. **Lack of Support for Spiritual Exploration:** - Due to strains on spiritual growth and harmony, there will be a lack of support for spiritual exploration. As stated in *Proverbs 27:17 ("As iron sharpens iron, so one person sharpens another"),* the importance of mutual

support in nurturing spiritual growth and maintaining harmony is encouraged.

5. **Spiritual Neglect and Busy Lifestyles:** - Strains may arise due to spiritual neglect in the midst of busy lifestyles. Mark 6:31 ("Come with me by yourselves to a quiet place and get some rest"), emphasizes the need for taking a breather and resting. This section advocates for intentional pauses to nurture spiritual growth of a couple amidst the demands of life.

6. **Unresolved Conflicts:** - Unresolved conflict often cause can strain growth and harmony. ***Matthew 18:15-17*** (*"If your brother or sister sins, go and point out their fault"*), encourages open communication and resolution to foster a spiritually harmonious environment.

This section addresses the strains that can hinder spiritual growth and harmony within intimate sacred connections. By examining these challenges through a spiritual lens and drawing from biblical insights, it offers guidance for individuals and couples seeking to navigate and overcome the obstacles that may impede their shared spiritual journey.

V. CHAPTER 4: BALANCING THE ENERGIES

This pivotal chapter explores the art of harmonizing and balancing spiritual energies within intimate sacred connections. It makes available practical insights and timeless wisdom to guide individuals and couples on a journey toward equilibrium in their spiritual dimensions. These practical insights include:

1. **Understanding Yin and Yang Energies:** - The chapter introduces the concept of Yin and Yang energies. ("In Chinese philosophy, yin and yang refer to **the complementary yet opposing forces that are both interconnected and interdependent. They represent opposites yet complementary energies**"). Drawing inspiration from *Ecclesiastes 3:1* *("There is a time for everything, and a season for every activity under the heavens").* This Biblical verse explores how embracing both receptive and active energies contributes to a balanced spiritual dynamic.

2. **Cultivating Mutual Spiritual Respect:** - Inspired by *Romans 12:10-("Be devoted to one another in love. Honor one another above yourselves"),* this section stresses the significance of mutual respect in balancing spiritual energies. It explores how cultivating respect creates a harmonious atmosphere for spiritual growth and deeper intimacy.

3. **Shared Spiritual Practices:** - To balance the spiritual energies the need for shared spiritual practices arises; aligning with *Matthew 18:20 ("For where two or three gather in my name, there am I with them").* It provides practical suggestions for couples to engage in spiritual rituals that enhance their connection and balance their

energies. Practices such as meditation, prayer and sacred reading can enhance spiritual connectedness.

4. **Harmonizing Individual Spiritual Journeys:** - As stated in *Ecclesiastes 4:9-10* (*"Two are better than one... If either of them falls down, one can help the other up"*), this section explores the art of harmonizing or balancing individual spiritual journeys within the context of a sacred relationship. It encourages partners to support each other's personal growth.

5. **Open Communication on Spiritual Needs:** - Inspired by *James 1:19* (*"My dear brothers and sisters, take note of this: Everyone should be quick to listen, slow to speak, and slow to become angry"*), this section guides couples in fostering open communication about their spiritual needs. It mentions how understanding and expressing these needs contribute to spiritual and harmonious balance.

6. **Energetic Alignment through Prayer:** - This section discusses the power of prayer in achieving energetic alignment. *Philippians 4:6-7* (*"Do not be anxious about anything, but in every situation, by prayer and petition, with thanksgiving, present your requests to God"*), calls for the need to present a couple requests to a higher power; it positions how prayer becomes a transformative tool for balance.

7. **Embracing Flexibility in Spiritual Practices:** - Inspired by *1 Corinthians 9:22* (*"I have become all things to all people so that by all possible means I might save some"*), this section encourages flexibility in spiritual practices. This verse notes how adapting to each other's spiritual preferences foster a dynamic and balanced spiritual atmosphere.

Balancing spiritual energies serves as a roadmap for individuals and couples to navigate the delicate art of balancing spiritual energies. By integrating practical strategies with timeless spiritual principles, it aims to empower readers to cultivate a harmonious and balanced spiritual connection within their relationships.

A. Cultivating Mindful and Sacred Sexuality

This transformative chapter explores the profound intersection of mindfulness and sacredness within the realm of human sexuality. Drawing on spiritual wisdom and mindfulness practices, it guides individuals and couples on a journey toward a deeper, more intentional, and sacred connection in their intimate lives. The following are ways couples can cultivate mindful and sacred sexuality:

1. **Mindful Presence in Intimacy:** - The chapter introduces the concept of mindful presence in intimate moments, aligning with *Song of Solomon 4:7 ("You are altogether beautiful, my love; there is no flaw in you")*. This explores how cultivating mindfulness enhances awareness, connection, and appreciation in the sacred dance of physical intimacy.

2. **Honoring the Sacred Temple:** - *1 Corinthians 6:19-20* calls the physical body as a temple of the Divine; *("Or do you not know that your body is a temple of the Holy Spirit within you?")*, the section delves into the sacred nature of the physical body. It guides individuals to honor and treat their bodies and their partner's body with reverence, fostering a deeper understanding of the sacredness within sexuality.

3. **Integrating Spirituality into Physical Connection:** - The chapter encourages the integration of spirituality into physical connection, Ephesians 5:31-32 states' ("Therefore a man shall leave his father and mother and hold fast to his wife, and the two shall become one flesh"). It explores how acknowledging the spiritual dimension enhances the depth and sacredness of the physical union.

4. **Mindful Communication in Intimate Relationships:** - Building on the importance of communication, the section emphasizes the role of mindful communication in intimate relationships. ***Proverbs 16:24*** encourages for the use of sweet words glazed with honey; *("Gracious words are like a honeycomb, sweetness to the soul and health to the body")*, This verse displays how mindful communication fosters connection and understanding.

5. **Exploration of Sensuality and Pleasure:** - The chapter encourages the exploration of sensuality and pleasure within the bounds of sacred intimacy. This section encourages individuals to approach physical pleasure as a sacred and shared experience. With the intention of balancing sensual energies, the couple is able to enjoy and indulge in extreme physical pleasure that transcends the natural.

6. **Sacred Rituals of Connection:** - This section explores the creation of sacred rituals of connection within intimate relationships. Aligning with ***Ecclesiastes 4:12*** *("A cord of three strands is not quickly broken")*, it emphasizes the significance of incorporating sacred practices that strengthen the bond between partners.

7. **Mindful Aftercare and Emotional Connection:** - The chapter discusses the importance of mindful aftercare and emotional connection following intimate moments. Referencing ***Colossians 3:14*** *("And above all these put on love, which binds everything together in perfect harmony")*. This verse further exposes how intentional care and emotional connection contribute to the sacredness of the shared spiritual experience.

8. **The Role of Gratitude in Sacred Sexuality:** - Building on the theme of gratitude, the section explores how expressing gratitude enhances sacred sexuality. ***1 Thessalonians 5:18*** encourages couple to be grateful for the shared experience; *("Give thanks in all circumstances; for this is the will of God in Christ Jesus for you")*, it encourages individuals to cultivate gratitude as a transformative element in their intimate sacred connection.

This section serves as a guide for individuals and couples to embark on a journey of cultivating mindful and sacred sexuality. By integrating mindfulness practices with spiritual principles, it aims to elevate the intimate connection to a sacred and profound experience, fostering a deeper understanding of the spiritual dimensions within human sexuality.

B. Practices for Maintaining Spiritual Alignment

This crucial section discovers practical and meaningful practices designed to help individuals and couples sustain spiritual alignment within the ebbs and flows of life. Rooted in timeless wisdom, the section provides actionable steps to foster a continuous connection with the divine and nurture the sacred aspects of relationships. These steps cover:

1. **Daily Spiritual Reflection:** - The step encourages the practice of daily spiritual reflection. Such reflections guide individuals to set aside moments for introspection, prayer, or meditation to align with spiritual guidance and insights.

2. Intentional Prayer Partnerships: - Building on the power of communal prayer, the section explores the concept of intentional prayer partnerships. Referencing *Matthew 18:20 ("For where two or three are gathered in my name, there am I among them"),* it encourages couples to form partnerships for shared prayers, enhancing spiritual alignment.

3. **Regular Participation in Sacred Rituals:** - The step emphasizes the importance of regular participation in sacred rituals, aligning with *Ecclesiastes 3:1 ("For everything there is a season, and a time for every matter under heaven").* It explores how consistently engaging in meaningful rituals fosters spiritual connection and aligns individuals with divine timing.

4. **Mindful Scripture Study and Meditation:** - Building on the wisdom found in scripture, the section encourages mindful scripture

study and meditation. As written in ***Joshua 1:8*** (*"This Book of the Law shall not depart from your mouth, but you shall meditate on it day and night"*), this verse guides couples to immerse themselves in sacred texts, meditating on them day and night for spiritual nourishment.

5. **Shared Acts of Service and Compassion:** - Inspired by ***Galatians 5:13*** (*"For you were called to freedom, brothers. Only do not use your freedom as an opportunity for the flesh, but through love serve one another"*), this step dictates how shared acts of service and compassion contribute to deeper spiritual alignment. It encourages couples to engage in charitable endeavors together.

6. **Nature-Based Spiritual Practices:** - This step suggests incorporating nature-based spiritual practices, aligning with ***Psalm 104:24-30*** (*"O Lord, how manifold are your works! In wisdom have you made them all"*. This verse explores how connecting with nature fosters a sense of awe and aligns individuals with the divine creation.

7. **Seasonal and Lunar Observances:** - Building on the cyclical nature of life, the section introduces the idea of seasonal and lunar observances. Referencing ***Ecclesiastes 3:2*** (*"A time to be born, and a time to die; a time to plant, and a time to pluck up what is planted"*), it guides couples to align their spiritual practices with natural rhythms.

8. Gratitude Journaling: - This step advocates for the practice of gratitude journaling; drawing from ***1 Thessalonians 5:18*** (*"Give thanks in all circumstances; for this is the will of God in Christ Jesus for you"*). It explores how expressing gratitude fosters a continuous alignment with the divine and enhances overall spiritual well-being.

All these steps serve as a practical guide for individuals and couples to maintain spiritual alignment through intentional practices. By incorporating these rituals into daily life, couples are encouraged to cultivate a consistent connection with the divine, fostering a resilient and sacred foundation for their spiritual journey.

C. Harmonizing the Physical and Spiritual Realms

In this transformative section, we look into the intricate dance between the physical and spiritual dimensions of our existence. Drawing wisdom from various spiritual traditions and practical insights, the chapter guides individuals and couples on a journey toward harmonizing the tangible and the divine aspects of life.

1. **The Sacred Unity of Body and Spirit**: - Rooted in the understanding of the body as a temple, the chapter explores the sacred unity of body and spirit. *1 Corinthians 6:19-20* reminds couples and individuals of the sanctity of their bodies *("Or do you not know that your body is a temple of the Holy Spirit within you?")*, it invites readers to honor the physical vessel as an integral part of their spiritual journey.

2. **Embodied Spirituality Practices**: - This section introduces embodied spirituality practices, aligning with *Romans 12:1-2 ("I appeal to you therefore, brothers, by the mercies of God, to present your bodies as a living sacrifice, holy and acceptable to God")*. It provides practical suggestions for integrating spiritual practices into daily activities, fostering a seamless connection between the physical and spiritual realms.

3. **Mindful Eating and Nourishment**: - Building on the concept of mindful living, the section explores mindful eating as a means of spiritual nourishment. Referencing *1 Corinthians 10:31 ("So, whether you eat or drink, or whatever you do, do all to the glory of God")*, which encourages individuals to approach nourishment with gratitude and deeper sense awareness.

4. **Sacred Movement and Exercise:** - Inspired by the idea of the body as a vehicle for spiritual expression, this section advocates for sacred movement and exercise. *1 Timothy 4:8* explores how physical activity can become a spiritual practice; *("For while bodily training is of some value, godliness is of value in every way").*

5. **Balancing Rest and Activity:** - The body as a temple should be taken care off and this section stresses the importance of balancing rest and activity, aligning with *Psalm 127:2 ("It is in vain that you rise up early and go late to rest, eating the bread of anxious toil; for he gives to his beloved sleep").* This biblical verse explores how embracing periods of rest contributes to spiritual harmony in the midst of life's activities.

6. **Sacred Sexuality and Intimacy:** - Building on the exploration of sacred sexuality, the section delves deeper into the intimate connection between the physical and spiritual realms in the context of romantic sacred relationships. Referencing *1 Corinthians 7:3-4 ("The husband should give to his wife her conjugal rights, and likewise the wife to her husband"),* it explores how physical intimacy can be a sacred and spiritually enriching experience.

7. Mindful Presence in Daily Tasks: - This section encourages mindful presence in daily tasks, aligning with *Colossians 3:17 ("And whatever you do, in word or deed, do everything in the name of the Lord Jesus, giving thanks to God the Father through him").* It guides couples to infuse everyday activities with spiritual awareness, creating a harmonious blend of the physical and spiritual.

8. **Holistic Wellness Practices**: - Inspired by the holistic approach to well-being, the section explores practices that address physical, mental, and spiritual aspects. *1 Thessalonians 5:23* states *("Now may the God of peace himself sanctify you completely, and may your whole spirit and soul and body be kept blameless"),* this guides couples and individuals towards a holistic approach to wellness.

In essence, Chapter 4 serves as a guide for individuals and couples seeking to harmonize the physical and spiritual realms. By embracing the sacredness inherent in the physical aspects of life and integrating spiritual practices into daily activities, readers are invited to create a unified and balanced existence where the tangible and the divine seamlessly coexist.

VI. CHAPTER 5: NAVIGATING CHALLENGES

In this pivotal chapter, we explore the inevitable challenges that arise within intimate connections and relationships. Drawing on practical insights and wisdom from various sources, the chapter serves as a guide for individuals and couples, offering strategies to navigate difficulties and emerge stronger in the face of adversity. The following actions help in navigating challenges and enhancing harmony in a sacred union:

1. **Embracing Vulnerability in Communication:** - Rooted in the understanding that communication is key, the chapter encourages individuals to embrace vulnerability in expressing their thoughts and feelings. It explores the transformative power of open and empathetic communication during challenging times.

2. Cultivating Patience and Understanding: - Inspired by *Ephesians 4:2 ("Be completely humble and gentle; be patient, bearing with one another in love")*, the section delves into the importance of cultivating patience and understanding. It provides practical insights on navigating challenges with a spirit of empathy and resilience.

3. **The Art of Active Listening:** - The chapter introduces the art of active listening, aligning with *James 1:19 ("Let every person be quick to hear, slow to speak, slow to anger")*. This guides couples on the transformative journey of truly hearing and understanding their partner's perspective, fostering a deeper connection in the midst of challenges.

4. **Seeking Guidance in Shared Values:** - Building on the foundation of shared values, the section explores how seeking guidance in alignment with those values can navigate challenges. Still referencing, *Amos 3:3 ("Can two walk together, unless they are agreed?")*, it encourages couples to find common ground based on their shared spiritual and ethical principles.

5. **Spiritual Reflection during Difficult Times:** - Drawing from *Psalm 34:17-18 ("When the righteous cry for help, the Lord hears and delivers them out of all their troubles")*, the chapter suggests incorporating spiritual reflection during difficult times. It explores how turning to spiritual practices and seeking divine guidance can provide solace and clarity.

6. **Forgiveness as a Healing Force:** - Inspired by *Colossians 3:13 ("Bear with each other and forgive one another if any of you has a grievance against someone. Forgive as the Lord forgave you")*, the section delves into the transformative power of forgiveness. It guides individuals on the path of letting go and fostering healing in the midst of challenges.

7. **Collaborative Problem-Solving:** - The chapter advocates for collaborative problem-solving, aligning with *Ecclesiastes 4:9-10 ("Two are better than one because they have a good return for their labor")*. It explores strategies for couples to work together, leveraging their strengths to overcome challenges and forge a resilient partnership.

8. **Turning Challenges into Growth Opportunities:** - Building on the idea that challenges can be catalysts for growth, the section encourages individuals to view difficulties as opportunities.

A. Recognizing and Addressing Spiritual Disconnect

In this pivotal section, we explore the nuances of spiritual disconnect within intimate relationships and provide practical insights on recognizing, understanding, and effectively addressing these challenges. Rooted in wisdom from various spiritual traditions, the chapter guides individuals and couples toward rekindling spiritual connection.

1. **Signs of Spiritual Disconnection:** - The section begins by elucidating common signs of spiritual disconnection, drawing inspiration from *1 Corinthians 7:5 ("Do not deprive each other except perhaps by mutual consent and for a time, so that you may devote yourselves to prayer")*. It encourages individuals to recognize subtle cues indicating a shift in spiritual alignment within the relationship.

2. **Open Dialogue on Spiritual Shifts**: - Building on the foundation of open communication, the section advocates for a candid dialogue about spiritual shifts. Referencing *Amos 3:3 ("Can two walk together, unless they are agreed?")*, it guides couples to express their evolving spiritual needs and beliefs, fostering an atmosphere of understanding.

3. **Individual Spiritual Reflection:** - Inspired by *Psalm 139:23-24 ("Search me, O God, and know my heart! Try me and know my thoughts!")*, the section emphasizes the importance of individual spiritual reflection. It encourages individuals to delve into their own beliefs and values, fostering self-awareness as a key component of addressing spiritual disconnect.

4. **Seeking Guidance from Spiritual Leaders:** - The section explores the role of seeking guidance from spiritual leaders during times of disconnect. Drawing from *Proverbs 11:14 ("For lack of guidance a nation falls, but victory is won through many advisers"),* it suggests involving wise counsel to navigate the complexities of spiritual shifts within the relationship.

5. **Revisiting Shared Spiritual Practices:** - Building on the idea of shared practices, the section advocates for revisiting and adapting shared spiritual rituals. Aligning with *Colossians 3:16 ("Let the word of Christ dwell in you richly"),* it encourages couples to explore new ways of connecting spiritually, ensuring that these practices evolve alongside the changes in their relationship and their shared higher values.

6. **Couples Retreats and Spiritual Renewal:** - Drawing inspiration from *Mark 6:31 ("Come with me by yourselves to a quiet place and get some rest"),* the section explores the rejuvenating impact of couples retreats and spiritual renewal. It suggests intentional pauses for reflection and reconnection, providing space for couples to realign spiritually.

7. **Forgiveness and Healing from Spiritual Dissonance:** - Inspired by *Ephesians 4:32 ("Be kind to one another, tenderhearted, forgiving one another, as God in Christ forgave you"),* the section delves into the transformative power of forgiveness. It guides couples through the process of healing from spiritual dissonance, fostering a renewed sense of compassion and understanding.

8. **Creating a Shared Spiritual Vision:** - The section concludes by encouraging couples to co-create a shared spiritual vision for their relationship. Referencing *Proverbs 29:18 ("Where there is no vision, the people perish"),* it emphasizes the importance of setting shared goals and aspirations that align with the evolving spiritual path of the couple.

This section serves as a guide for recognizing and addressing spiritual disconnect within intimate relationships. By fostering open communication, self-reflection, seeking guidance, and adapting shared practices, individuals and couples are equipped with the tools to navigate and transcend spiritual challenges, ultimately fostering a deeper and more resilient spiritual connection.

B. Seeking Guidance and Support

In this crucial section, we explore the transformative power of seeking guidance and support within the context of intimate sacred connections. Entrenched in spiritual wisdom and practical insights, the section serves as a compass for individuals and couples navigating the complexities of relationships, offering avenues for seeking external assistance.

1. **The Role of Spiritual Mentors:** - Drawing from *Proverbs 13:20* (*"Walk with the wise and become wise, for a companion of fools suffers harm"*), the section highlights the significance of spiritual mentors. It explores how seeking guidance from experienced and wise individuals can provide valuable insights for navigating challenges and fostering spiritual growth.

2. **Counseling and Therapy Services:** - The section delves into the realm of professional counseling and therapy services, aligning with *Proverbs 15:22* (*"Plans fail for lack of counsel, but with many advisers, they succeed"*). It guides individuals and couples to consider professional support as a constructive means of addressing relational challenges and fostering healing.

3. **Community and Support Networks:** - Building on the idea of communal support, the chapter explores the role of community and support networks. *Ecclesiastes 4:9-10* states (*"Two are better than one because they have a good return for their labor"*), this inspires individuals to lean on trusted friends, family, or spiritual communities for guidance and encouragement.

4. **Retreats and Spiritual Gatherings:** - Inspired by *Matthew 18:20* (*"For where two or three gather in my name, there am I with them"*), the section advocates for participation in retreats and spiritual gatherings. It explores how immersing oneself in a collective spiritual environment can provide a rejuvenating and supportive backdrop for relationship growth.

5. **Books and Resources on Relationship Dynamics:** - The section suggests turning to books and resources focused on relationship dynamics, drawing from *Proverbs 19:20* (*"Listen to advice and accept discipline, and at the end, you will be counted among the wise"*). It guides individuals and couples to explore literature that offers valuable insights and practical wisdom for navigating the intricacies of intimate connections.

6. **Spiritual Communities and Congregations:** - Building on the foundation of shared spiritual values, the section explores the benefits of engaging with spiritual communities and congregations. Aligning with *Hebrews 10:25* (*"Not giving up meeting together, as some are in the habit of doing, but encouraging one another"*), it emphasizes the support found in a communal spiritual journey.

7. Online Support Forums and Groups: - The section acknowledges the influence of the digital age and suggests exploring online support forums and groups. Drawing from *Galatians 6:2* (*"Carry each other's burdens, and in this way, you will fulfill the law of Christ"*), it highlights the potential for finding virtual support and guidance tailored to specific relationship challenges.

8. **Prayer Partnerships and Intercession:** -Inspired by the power of prayer partnerships, the section encourages couples to engage in mutual intercession. Referencing *James 5:16* (*"Therefore confess your sins to each other and pray for each other so that you may be healed. The prayer of a righteous person is powerful and effective"*), it explores the transformative impact of shared spiritual practices within the relationship.

This section serves as a comprehensive guide for individuals and couples seeking guidance and support in their intimate connections. By considering a diverse range of sources, from mentors and counseling services to community engagement and online forums, individuals are empowered to proactively seek the support needed for a thriving and resilient relationship.

C.Transformative Approaches to Overcome Obstacles

In this vital section, we delve into transformative approaches designed to empower individuals and couples to overcome obstacles within their relationships. Taking on both practical strategies and spiritual insights, this section serves as a guide for navigating challenges and fostering growth amidst adversity.

1. **Mindful Communication in Conflict Resolution:** - Rooted in the wisdom of *Proverbs 15:1 ("A gentle answer turns away wrath, but a harsh word stirs up anger")*, the chapter explores the transformative power of mindful communication. It provides practical techniques for navigating conflicts with empathy and openness, fostering understanding and resolution.

2. **Cultivating Resilience through Shared Spirituality:** - Building on the idea of shared spirituality, the section delves into how cultivating resilience can be rooted in a common spiritual foundation. *Philippians 4:13* states,*("I can do all things through him who strengthens me")*, this encourages individuals and couples to find strength in their shared beliefs during challenging times.

3. **Mindfulness Practices for Emotional Regulation:** - Inspired by the concept of mindfulness, the chapter introduces practices for emotional regulation during obstacles. Referencing *James 1:19 ("Let every person be quick to hear, slow to speak, slow to anger")*, it guides individuals in incorporating mindfulness techniques to manage emotions and respond thoughtfully in challenging situations.

4. **Forgiveness as a Path to Healing:** - The section explores the transformative nature of forgiveness, drawing from *Colossians 3:13* *("Bear with each other and forgive one another if any of you has a grievance against someone. Forgive as the Lord forgave you")*. This guides individuals on the journey of forgiveness as a catalyst for healing and renewed connection.

5. **Building Trust through Transparency:** - Rooted in the principle of transparency, the section promotes the building of trust as a transformative approach. Based on *Proverbs 11:3* *("The integrity of the upright guides them, but the unfaithful are destroyed by their duplicity")*, this verse shows the impact of honesty and openness in rebuilding trust after facing obstacles.

6. **Empowering Growth through Adversity:** - Inspired by *Romans 5:3-4* *("Not only so, but we also glory in our sufferings, because we know that suffering produces perseverance; perseverance, character; and character, hope")*, the section explores how adversity can be a catalyst for personal and relational growth. It encourages individuals and couples to view challenges as opportunities for transformative change.

7. Rekindling Intimacy with Deliberate Acts of Love: - Building on the importance of intimacy, the chapter suggests deliberate acts of love to rekindle connection. Aligning with *Song of Solomon 6:3* *("I am my beloved's and my beloved is mine")*, it provides practical suggestions for fostering emotional and physical intimacy during challenging phases.

8. **Spiritual Rituals for Renewal:** - The section concludes by introducing spiritual rituals for renewal, drawing inspiration from *Isaiah 40:31* *("But those who hope in the Lord will renew their strength")*. This serves as a guide for individuals and couples in creating intentional spiritual practices to renew their connection and find strength during times of obstacles.

This section serves as a roadmap for individuals and couples seeking transformative approaches to overcome obstacles in their relationships. By integrating mindfulness, shared spirituality, forgiveness, trust-building, and intentional acts of love, individuals are equipped with tools to not only navigate challenges but also emerge from them with strengthened bonds and a renewed sense of connection.

VII. CHAPTER 6: TOOLS FOR SPIRITUAL GROWTH

In the context of sacred union in relations, practices like partner meditation, deep communication, shared spiritual exploration, and collaborative rituals can foster a deeper connection and spiritual growth between partners. Exploring meditation, reading sacred texts, practicing mindfulness and engaging in reflective journaling can be effective tools for spiritual growth.

A.Meditation and Prayer Practices

This section explores the profound impact of meditation and prayer as integral tools for spiritual growth within the realm of intimate relationships. Drawing on both ancient wisdom and contemporary insights, this section serves as a guide for individuals and couples seeking to cultivate a deep and transformative spiritual connection through intentional practices.

1. **Mindful Breathing Meditation:** - Rooted in the essence of mindfulness, the section introduces mindful breathing meditation. Building on the breath as a focal point, it aligns with Psalm 46:10 *("Be still and know that I am God")*, guiding individuals to cultivate inner stillness and awareness through intentional breath-work.

2. **Loving-Kindness Meditation for Compassion:** - The section explores the transformative power of loving-kindness meditation, drawing inspiration from Matthew 22:39 *("Love your neighbor as yourself")*. It encourages individuals to extend feelings of love and compassion not only to oneself but also to their partner, fostering a deeper sense of empathy and connection.

3. **Centering Prayer for Spiritual Grounding:** - Inspired by the practice of centering prayer, the section delves into techniques for spiritual grounding. Referencing **Colossians 3:2** *("Set your minds on things above, not on earthly things")*, this guides couples and individuals to find a centered space within, fostering a connection with the divine and transcending daily challenges.

4. **Gratitude Prayer for Relationship Blessings:** - Building on the power of gratitude, the section introduces a gratitude prayer specifically

tailored for relationship blessings. *1 Thessalonians 5:18 ("Give thanks in all circumstances");* encourages couples to express gratitude for each other and the shared experiences that contribute to their spiritual journey.

5. **Visualization Meditation for Shared Goals:** - The section explores the practice of visualization meditation, aligning with *Proverbs 29:18 ("Where there is no vision, the people perish").* This guides individuals and couples to visualize and align their spiritual and relational goals, fostering a shared vision that propels them forward on their journey.

6. **Bible Verse Meditation for Spiritual Insight:** - Drawing from the rich wisdom of scripture, the section introduces Bible verse meditation for spiritual insight. Referencing *Psalm 119:105 ("Your word is a lamp to my feet and a light to my path"),* this guides individuals to reflect on and internalize specific verses that resonate with their spiritual aspirations.

7. **Silent Prayer for Deep Connection:** - The section advocates for the practice of silent prayer, aligning with *1 Kings 19:12 ("And after the earthquake a fire, but the Lord was not in the fire; and after the fire a still small voice").* It encourages individuals and couples to engage in moments of profound silence, fostering a deep connection with the Divine and each other.

8. **Guided Couple's Prayer for Unity**: - Inspired by the concept of unity, the section introduces guided couple's prayer. Building on *Ecclesiastes 4:12 ("A cord of three strands is not quickly broken"),* this notion guides couples through a shared prayer experience, fostering unity and a sense of interconnectedness in their spiritual journey.

This section serves as a comprehensive guide to meditation and prayer practices tailored for spiritual growth within intimate sacred relationships. By incorporating these practices into their daily lives, individuals and couples can embark on a transformative journey, deepening their spiritual connection and creating a sacred space for mutual growth and understanding.

B.Rituals and Ceremonies for Spiritual Connection

In this transformative section, we explore the significance of rituals and ceremonies as potent vehicles for nurturing spiritual connection within intimate sacred relationships. Harnessing the power of symbolism and shared experiences, this section serves as a guide for individuals and couples seeking to enrich their spiritual journey through intentional practices.

1. **Daily Blessing Rituals:** - Rooted in the idea of daily intentionality, the section introduces daily blessing rituals. Inspired by *Numbers 6:24-26* (*"The Lord bless you and keep you; the Lord make his face shine on you and be gracious to you; the Lord turn his face toward you and give you peace"*), encourages couples to start or end their day with words of blessing for each other.

2. **Sacred Mealtime Ceremonies:** - The section explores the transformative nature of sacred mealtime ceremonies, aligning with *Matthew 26:26-28* (*"While they were eating, Jesus took bread, and when he had given thanks, he broke it and gave it to his disciples, saying, 'Take and eat; this is my body'"*). It guides couples in infusing their shared meals with gratitude and reverence, fostering a sense of spiritual communion.

3. **Candlelit Connection Rituals:** - Building on the symbolism of light, the chapter introduces candlelit connection rituals. This encourages couples to create moments of intimacy and reflection illuminated by candlelight, enhancing the spiritual ambiance of their shared space.

4. **Seasonal Celebrations and Reflections:** - Inspired by the changing seasons, the section explores the practice of seasonal celebrations and reflections. Referencing *Ecclesiastes 3:1* *("There is a time for everything, and a season for every activity under the heavens")*, this biblical verse encourages couples to mark significant life events and seasonal transitions with intentional ceremonies, fostering a sense of continuity and spiritual growth.

5. **Renewal Ceremonies for Relationship Milestones:** - The section delves into the transformative impact of renewal ceremonies for relationship milestones, aligning with *2 Corinthians 5:17* *("Therefore, if anyone is in Christ, the new creation has come: The old has gone, the new is here!")*. It guides couples in creating ceremonies to renew vows, celebrate anniversaries, and acknowledge transformative moments in their journey.

6. **Nature-based Rituals for Grounding:** - Drawing inspiration from the beauty of nature, the section introduces nature-based rituals for grounding. Building on *Psalm 19:1* *("The heavens declare the glory of God; the skies proclaim the work of his hands")*, this verse encourages couples to engage in rituals that connect them with the natural world, fostering a sense of awe and spiritual grounding.

7. **Shared Prayer Walks or Meditative Strolls:** - The section advocates for the practice of shared prayer walks or meditative strolls, aligning with *Proverbs 3:6* *("In all your ways submit to him, and he will make your paths straight")*. This guides couples to engage in intentional walks, combining physical movement with spiritual connection, fostering a harmonious balance.

8. **Creation of Personal Spiritual Altars:** - Inspired by the concept of sacred space, the section introduces the creation of personal spiritual altars. Drawing from *Joshua 24:15* *("As for me and my household, we will serve the Lord")*; this verse guides individuals and couples to curate sacred spaces within their homes, filled with symbolic items that hold spiritual significance.

This section serves as a guide to rituals and ceremonies for fostering spiritual connection within intimate relationships. By infusing daily life with intentional practices, couples can create a sacred tapestry of shared experiences, deepening their spiritual bond and enriching their journey together.

C. Incorporating Spiritual Wisdom into Intimate Connections.

This section explores the integration of spiritual wisdom into the fabric of intimate connections. By means of timeless insights from various spiritual traditions, this section serves as a guide for individuals and couples seeking to infuse their relationships with depth, meaning, and a transcendent understanding.

1. **Mindful Presence in Intimate Moments:** - Rooted in the essence of presence, this section advocates for mindful awareness during intimate moments. *1 Corinthians 6:19-20 ("Do you not know that your bodies are temples of the Holy Spirit?")*; guides individuals to approach physical intimacy with reverence and an awareness of the spiritual connection between partners.

2. **Spiritual Alignment in Shared Values**: - Building on the foundation of shared values, the section explores the importance of spiritual alignment. Still referencing *Amos 3:3 ("Can two walk together, unless they are agreed?")*, it encourages couples to continually assess and reinforce their shared spiritual principles as a guiding force in their relationship.

3. **Wisdom from Proverbs for Communication:** - The section delves into the wisdom of Proverbs for effective communication within intimate connections. Drawing from *Proverbs 15:1 ("A gentle answer turns away wrath, but a harsh word stirs up anger")*, this verse provides insights on cultivating kindness and wisdom in verbal exchanges, fostering understanding and harmony.

4. **Sacred Rituals for Emotional Connection:** - Inspired by the sacred, the section introduces rituals for emotional connection. Aligning with *Ecclesiastes 4:12 ("A cord of three strands is not quickly broken")*, it guides couples to create rituals that symbolize their emotional bond, fostering a sense of sacred unity in their shared experiences.

5. **Principles of Compassion in Conflict Resolution:** - Building on the principle of compassion, the chapter explores spiritual approaches to conflict resolution. Drawing from *Matthew 18:21-22 ("Lord, how often shall my brother sin against me, and I forgive him? Up to seven times?")*, this verse guides individuals to approach conflicts with a compassionate heart, fostering forgiveness and healing.

6. **Integrating Patience and Understanding:** - The section advocates for the integration of patience and understanding, aligning with *Ephesians 4:2 ("Be completely humble and gentle; be patient, bearing with one another in love")*. It explores how embodying these virtues can transform challenges into opportunities for growth and deepened connection.

7. **Wisdom from Psalms for Emotional Expression:** - Drawing from the emotional depth of Psalms, the section introduces wisdom for emotional expression. Referencing *Psalm 34:17-18 ("When the righteous cry for help, the Lord hears and delivers them out of all their troubles")*, this verse boldly encourages individuals and couples to express their emotions authentically, trusting in the power of divine understanding.

8. **Applying Spiritual Parables to Relationship Dynamics:** - Inspired by spiritual parables, the section explores their application to relationship dynamics. Drawing from parables such as the Prodigal Son or the Good Samaritan, the Bible guides individuals to glean profound insights and lessons for compassion, forgiveness, and unconditional love within their intimate connections.

This section serves as a compass for incorporating spiritual wisdom into intimate connections. By infusing daily interactions, conflicts, and shared moments with spiritual insights, individuals and couples can navigate their relationship journey with depth, wisdom, and a profound understanding of the sacred nature of their connection.

VIII. CHAPTER 7: EMBRACING DIVINE WISDOM

In this transcendent chapter, we explore the profound journey of embracing divine wisdom within the context of intimate sacred connections. Rooted in spiritual insights and guided by the wisdom of various traditions, this chapter serves as a beacon for individuals and couples seeking to deepen their understanding of divine principles within their sacred relationships.

1. Surrendering to Divine Guidance: - The section begins by emphasizing the transformative power of surrendering to divine guidance. Drawing inspiration from *Proverbs 3:5-6* (*"Trust in the Lord with all your heart and lean not on your own understanding; in all your ways submit to him, and he will make your paths straight"*), it guides individuals to trust in a higher wisdom beyond their own.

2. **Practicing Spiritual Discernment:** - Laying a foundation on the concept of discernment, the section explores the practice of spiritual discernment within relationships. Referencing *1 John 4:1* (*"Dear friends, do not believe every spirit, but test the spirits to see whether they are from God"*), this verse exhorts couples and individuals to seek divine insight in discerning the path of their intimate connections.

3. **Divine Timing in Relationship Milestones:** - The section delves into the notion of divine timing for relationship milestones. Drawing from *Ecclesiastes 3:1* (*"There is a time for everything, and a season for every activity under the heavens"*), this verse encourages individuals to trust in divine orchestration for significant moments in their relationship journey.

4. **Aligning with Universal Love Principles:** - Inspired by the universality of love, the section introduces the concept of aligning with universal love principles. *1 Corinthians 13:4-7 ("Love is patient, love is kind...")*, acts as a guide to individuals and couples to embody divine love as a guiding force in their interactions, fostering a sacred atmosphere within their connection.

5. **Wisdom from Sacred Texts for Decision-Making:** - Drawing from sacred texts, the chapter explores the wisdom inherent in these texts for decision-making. Referencing *James 1:5 ("If any of you lacks wisdom, you should ask God, who gives generously to all without finding fault")*, it encourages seeking divine guidance in decisions that impact the course of intimate sacred relationships.

6. **Cultivating the Fruits of the Spirit:** - Building on the fruits of the Spirit, the section delves into *Galatians 5:22-23 ("But the fruit of the Spirit is love, joy, peace, forbearance, kindness, goodness, faithfulness, gentleness, and self-control")*. It guides couples and individuals to cultivate these virtues, creating a fertile ground for the presence of divine wisdom in their relationships.

7. **Prayer for Relationship Blessings:** - The section introduces the practice of prayer specifically tailored for relationship blessings. Drawing from *Matthew 18:19-20 ("Again, truly I tell you that if two of you on earth agree about anything they ask for, it will be done for them by my Father in heaven")*, it guides individuals and couples to invoke divine blessings into their relationships through prayer.

8. **Living in Harmony with Divine Purpose:** - Inspired by the concept of divine purpose, the section explores living in harmony with the purpose that transcends individual desires. Drawing from *Jeremiah 29:11 ("For I know the plans I have for you, plans to prosper you and not to harm you, plans to give you hope and a future")*, it encourages individuals to align their relationships with a broader, divine purpose.

This section serves as a guide for individuals and couples seeking to embrace divine wisdom within the sacred space of their intimate connections. By surrendering to divine guidance, practicing discernment, and aligning with universal principles of love, individuals can embark on a transformative journey of deepening their spiritual connection within their relationships.

A.Integrating Spiritual Principles into Daily Life

In this section, we explore practical ways to seamlessly integrate spiritual principles into the tapestry of daily life. Rooted in wisdom from various spiritual traditions, this section serves as a guide for individuals and couples aspiring to embody their spiritual values in the mundane moments of everyday existence.

1. **Morning Rituals for Spiritual Alignment:** - The section begins by exploring morning rituals that set the tone for spiritual alignment throughout the day. Drawing inspiration from ***Psalm 143:8*** *("Let the morning bring me word of your unfailing love, for I have put my trust in you"),* it suggests practices like prayer, meditation, or affirmations to align with spiritual principles at the start of each day.

2. **Mindful Presence in Daily Activities:** - Building on the foundation of mindfulness, the section encourages the practice of mindful presence in daily activities. Aligning with ***Colossians 3:23*** *("Whatever you do, work at it with all your heart, as working for the Lord"),* it guides individuals to infuse ordinary tasks with spiritual consciousness and a sense of purpose.

3. **Sacred Mealtime Connections:** - The section delves into the transformative potential of turning mealtime into a sacred connection. Inspired by *1 Corinthians 10:31 ("So whether you eat or drink or whatever you do, do it all for the glory of God"),* it suggests incorporating gratitude, reflection, or prayer into mealtime, fostering a sense of divine connection.

4. **Evening Reflections for Spiritual Growth**: - Drawing from the concept of reflection, the section introduces evening practices for spiritual growth. Referencing *Psalm 119:15* *("I meditate on your precepts and consider your ways")*, it encourages individuals and couples to reflect on their day, expressing gratitude and seeking insights for spiritual development.

5. **Prayerful Communication in Relationships:** - Building on the importance of communication, the section explores prayerful communication within relationships. *Ephesians 4:29* states ("Do not let any unwholesome talk come out of your mouths, but only what is helpful for building others up according to their needs"), this verse guides individuals to infuse conversations with kindness and a spiritual perspective.

6. **Acts of Kindness Rooted in Love:** - Inspired by the principle of love, the section encourages acts of kindness rooted in spiritual love. Drawing from *1 John 4:7* *("Dear friends, let us love one another, for love comes from God")*, it guides individuals to express love through compassionate actions, creating a ripple effect of positive energy in daily interactions.

7. **Scripture as a Guiding Light:** - This section advocates for using scripture as a guiding light throughout the day. Referencing *Psalm 119:105* *("Your word is a lamp for my feet, a light on my path")*, it suggests carrying verses or affirmations, turning to them in moments of decision or challenge, and allowing scripture to illuminate the path forward.

8. **Mindful Rest and Sabbath Moments:** - Building on the importance of rest, the section introduces the concept of mindful rest and Sabbath moments. Drawing from *Exodus 20:8* *("Remember the Sabbath day by keeping it holy")*, it encourages individuals to incorporate intentional moments of rest, reflection, and spiritual rejuvenation into their weekly routines.

In principle, this section serves as a guide for seamlessly integrating spiritual principles into the fabric of daily life. By infusing ordinary moments with intentionality, mindfulness, and a commitment to spiritual values, individuals and couples can create a sacred and harmonious rhythm in their everyday existence.

In the journey of integrating spiritual principles into daily life, each day becomes an opportunity to weave the sacred into the mundane. Starting the morning with intentional rituals, be it through prayer, meditation, or affirmations, sets a tone of spiritual alignment. Throughout the day, mindful presence transforms ordinary activities into moments of divine connection, whether in the workplace, at home, or during daily chores. Mealtime becomes more than sustenance, evolving into a sacred connection with gratitude and reflection. Evening reflections offer a space for spiritual growth, allowing individuals to express gratitude and seek insights. In relationships, communication takes on a prayerful dimension, and acts of kindness are rooted in spiritual love. Scripture becomes a guiding light in decision-making moments, and intentional rest periods create Sabbath moments of reflection and rejuvenation. This seamless integration of spiritual principles brings a sense of purpose, mindfulness, and divine connection into the very fabric of daily existence.

B.Upholding Reverence for the Sacred Essence of Sex

This section delves into the profound exploration of upholding reverence for the sacred essence of sex within the context of intimate sacred relationships. Rooted in spiritual insights and guided by a deep respect for the sacred nature of human connection, this section serves as a guide for individuals and couples seeking to honor the divine dimension and intention of their sexual experiences. Couples uphold the reverence of their sacred union through the following key aspects:

1. **Sacred Communication in Intimate Dialogues:** - The section begins by emphasizing the significance of sacred communication in intimate dialogues. ***Song of Solomon 4:7*** *("You are altogether beautiful, my love; there is no flaw in you");* guides individuals and couples to approach sexual discussions with openness, respect, and a recognition of the sacred beauty within each partner.

2. **Mindful Connection in Physical Intimacy:** - Building on the foundation of mindfulness, the section explores the practice of mindful connection in physical intimacy. ***1 Corinthians 6:19-20*** *("Your bodies are temples of the Holy Spirit");* reminds couples to revere the essence of their physical bodies as temples of the Divine. This encourages individuals and couples to engage in intimate moments with present awareness, acknowledging the sacred nature of their bodies and the connection they share.

3. **Shared Spiritual Practices for Intimacy:** - The section brings to light the transformative potential of shared spiritual practices for

intimacy. ***Ephesians 5:21-*** *("Submit to one another out of reverence for Christ");* here couples and individuals are encouraged to incorporate prayer, meditation, or other spiritual rituals into the intimate space, fostering a shared connection that transcends the physical.

4. **Understanding the Spiritual Symbolism of Sacred Union:** - Drawing from spiritual symbolism, the section introduces an exploration of the deeper meaning of union. Referencing ***Genesis 2:24*** *("Therefore a man shall leave his father and his mother and hold fast to his wife, and they shall become one flesh"),* it guides individuals to understand and honor the spiritual symbolism inherent in the physical union of partners.

5. **Cultivating Emotional and Spiritual Intimacy**: - Building on the concept of intimacy, the chapter advocates for cultivating emotional and spiritual intimacy alongside the physical. Aligning *with **Proverbs 4:23** ("Above all else, guard your heart, for everything you do flows from it"),* it encourages individuals and couples to nurture a deep connection that encompasses emotional, spiritual, and physical dimensions.

6. **Practicing Gratitude for the Gift of Intimacy:** - Inspired by the principle of gratitude, the section encourages the practice of gratitude for the gift of intimacy. This guides individuals and couples to express gratitude for the sacred and intimate connection they share, fostering a sense of appreciation for the divine gift of physical closeness.

7. **Honoring Boundaries with Reverence:** - The section explores the importance of honoring boundaries with reverence. Referencing ***1 Corinthians 7:3-5*** *("The husband should fulfill his marital duty to his wife, and likewise the wife to her husband"),* it emphasizes the mutual respect and communication required to establish and honor boundaries, ensuring a space of safety and sacredness.

8. **Seeking Spiritual Guidance in Sexual Challenges:** - Building on the notion of seeking guidance, the section introduces the concept of seeking spiritual guidance in the face of sexual challenges. ***James 1:5***

("If any of you lacks wisdom, let him ask God"), encourages individuals and couples to turn to spiritual principles for wisdom and understanding during times of difficulty or confusion.

This section widely serves as a compass for individuals and couples navigating the sacred essence of sex within their relationships. By upholding reverence, practicing mindful connection, and recognizing the spiritual dimensions of intimacy, individuals can embark on a transformative journey that honors the divine nature of the profound and sacred union they share.

C.Embracing Positive Transformations

Continuing the exploration of positive transformations within the sacred context of intimate connections, this section focuses on the journey of personal and relational growth. Steered by spiritual principles, individuals and couples embark on a transformative path that nurtures a deeper understanding of themselves, their partners, and the divine nature woven into their relationships. Here are a few guiding principles:

1. **Personal Evolution through Reflection:** - The chapter begins by highlighting the significance of personal evolution through spiritual reflection. Drawing inspiration from *2 Corinthians 3:18* (*"And we all, who with unveiled faces contemplate the Lord's glory, are being transformed into his image with ever-increasing glory"*), it encourages individuals to engage in self-reflection as a catalyst for positive notable personal transformations.

2. **Mutual Growth in Sacred Partnership:** - Building on the concept of partnership, the section explores mutual growth within sacred relationships. Aligning with *Ecclesiastes 4:9-10* (*"Two are better than one, because they have a good return for their labor"*), it guides couples to embrace their shared journey as an opportunity for mutual transformation, fostering a dynamic partnership rooted in spiritual principles.

3. **Resilience through Spiritual Principles:** - The section delves into the resilience cultivated through spiritual principles. Inspired by *Psalm 46:1* (*"God is our refuge and strength, an ever-present help in trouble"*), it explores how individuals and couples can draw on spiritual

principles to navigate challenges, fostering resilience and fortitude in the face of adversity.

4. **The Power of Forgiveness in Healing:** - Forgiveness is the key principle to healing. Drawing from the transformative power of forgiveness, the section introduces its role in the healing process. Referencing *Colossians 3:13* (*"Bear with each other and forgive one another if any of you has a grievance against someone. Forgive as the Lord forgave you"*), it guides individuals and couples to embrace forgiveness as a catalyst for positive transformation and healing. Forgiveness births the process of restoration and renewal in the sacred relationship.

5. **Spiritual Practices for Emotional Wellbeing:** - Building on the importance of emotional wellbeing, this section advocates for incorporating spiritual practices into daily life. Couples and individuals are encouraged to turn to spiritual practices for emotional balance and inner peace.

6. **Gratitude as a Transformative Mindset**: - Inspired by the transformative mindset of gratitude, the section explores its impact on personal and relational growth. *1 Thessalonians 5:18* encourages individuals and couples to cultivate a grateful mindset, fostering positive transformations in their outlook on life and relationships.

7. **Balancing Spirituality and Practicality:** - This section further emphasizes the importance of balancing spirituality and practicality in the transformative journey. Referencing *James 2:26* (*"As the body without the spirit is dead, so faith without deeds is dead"*), this serves as guide to individuals and couples to integrate spiritual principles into practical aspects of daily life, creating a harmonious blend that supports positive transformations.

8. **Aligning with Higher Purpose and Calling:** - Building on the concept of higher purpose, the section encourages individuals to align with their divine calling. Inspired by *Jeremiah 29:11* (*"For I know the plans I have for you, plans to prosper you and not to harm you, plans to give you hope and a future"*), this guides individuals and couples alike

to seek and embrace their unique purpose within the context of their relationships.

This section serves as a guide for individuals and couples embracing positive transformations within the sacred realm of their connections. By fostering personal evolution, mutual growth, resilience, forgiveness, and gratitude, individuals embark on a journey that not only enriches their own lives but contributes to the transformative tapestry of their intimate relationships.

IX. CONCLUSION

In concluding our exploration of "Sacred Union: Nurturing Spiritual Connections in Intimate Relationships," we stand at the culmination of a profound journey. This book has is a guide to unlocking the spiritual dimensions of intimacy, weaving together the threads of reverence, daily integration of spiritual principles, and the transformative power of positive growth.

As we reflect on the essence of the sacred within intimate connections, the significance of upholding reverence for the sacred essence of sex has been illuminated. This chapter laid the foundation for approaching physical intimacy with communication, mindfulness, shared spiritual practices, and an understanding of the deep symbolism inherent in the union of partners. It has urged individuals and couples to engage in the dance of intimacy with respect, mindfulness, and an acknowledgment of the divine woven into every moment.

The sacred union is not confined to physicality; it transcends the realms of the everyday, inviting individuals and couples to nurture a connection that spans the spiritual, emotional, and physical dimensions. The chapters have served as a roadmap for this journey, emphasizing the importance of weaving spirituality into the fabric of daily existence, fostering a harmonious balance between the practical and the divine.

May the insights shared in "Sacred Union" serve as a compass for those seeking a deeper connection within their intimate relationships. As we conclude this journey, the invitation resonates: to cultivate reverence, to integrate spiritual principles into the tapestry of daily life, and to embrace positive transformations as an ongoing process of growth and enlightenment. In the sacred union, we find not only a connection with our partners but a profound communion with the Divine within and around us.

A.Summarizing Key Points

1. **Reverence for the Sacred Essence of Sex:** - Communication, mindfulness, and shared spiritual practices are crucial for upholding reverence in intimate relationships. Understanding the deep symbolism in the physical union of partners fosters a sacred approach to intimacy.

2. **Positive Transformations within Relationships**: - Personal evolution, mutual growth, resilience, forgiveness, and gratitude are catalysts for positive transformations. - The integration of spiritual principles into daily life creates a harmonious rhythm, turning ordinary moments into sacred experiences.

3. **Integration of Spiritual Principles into Daily Life:** - Morning rituals, mindful presence, sacred mealtime connections, and evening reflections contribute to daily spiritual integration. - Prayerful communication, acts of kindness, and scripture as a guiding light enhance the practical aspects of daily life with spiritual principles.

4. **Embracing Divine Wisdom:** - Surrendering to divine guidance, practicing spiritual discernment, and aligning with universal love principles form a foundation for embracing divine wisdom. - Living in harmony with divine purpose and seeking guidance through prayer contribute to a spiritually aligned life.

5. **Clarity and Intention in Prayer:** - Choosing a quiet location, maintaining clarity in intentional prayer, and focusing on specificity enhance the efficacy of prayer. -Aligning prayer with values, using scripture, and expressing gratitude contribute to a meaningful and intentional prayer life.

6. **Exploration of the Spiritual Dimensions of Sex:** - Understanding the spiritual essence of sex involves exploring the sacred connection, embracing positive consequences, and recognizing the divine in intimate connections. -Acknowledging the potential negative consequences prompts a balanced and holistic exploration of the spiritual dimensions of sex.

7. **Incorporating Spiritual Wisdom into Intimate Connections:** - Mindful presence in intimate moments, aligning with shared values, and incorporating wisdom from sacred texts contribute to the infusion of spiritual wisdom. -Applying spiritual parables to relationship dynamics and integrating spiritual insights into daily interactions enriches intimate connections.

8. **Tools for Spiritual Growth:** - Personal and relational growth is facilitated through practices like prayer, meditation, rituals, and incorporating spiritual wisdom into intimate connections. -Embracing divine wisdom, aligning with universal love principles, and seeking spiritual guidance contribute to an ongoing journey of spiritual growth.

9. **Conclusion: The Sacred Union:** - The book concludes with an emphasis on the sacred journey, integrating spiritual principles into daily life, and embracing positive transformations within intimate relationships. - Upholding reverence, fostering personal and mutual growth, and balancing practicality with spirituality contribute to the sacred union within intimate connections.

B. Encouragement for Spiritual Growth and Balance

Embarking on a journey of spiritual growth and balance is a profound endeavor that enriches every facet of life. As you traverse this path, consider the following words of encouragement:

1. **Embrace the Journey:** - Spiritual growth is a lifelong journey, not a destination. Embrace the process, savor each step, and allow yourself the grace to evolve at your own pace.

2. **Cultivate Daily Practices:** - Integrate small, meaningful practices into your daily routine. Whether it's a moment of prayer, meditation, or gratitude, these practices create a consistent thread of spirituality in your life.

3. **Celebrate Progress, Not Perfection:** - Spiritual growth is about progress, not perfection. Celebrate the small victories, and don't be too hard on yourself during moments of perceived setbacks. Each experience holds a lesson.

4. **Seek Connection with others:** - Surround yourself with a supportive community. Share your journey, exchange insights, and learn from others. Connection with like-minded individuals can provide encouragement and diverse perspectives.

5. **Balance Spirituality with Practicality:** - Integrate spiritual principles into your everyday life. Let your spiritual beliefs guide your actions and decisions, finding a harmonious balance between the practical and the divine.

6. **Find Solace in Nature:** - Nature has a profound way of reconnecting us with our spiritual essence. Take moments to immerse

yourself in the beauty of the natural world, allowing it to inspire and ground you.

7. **Practice Mindfulness:** - Cultivate mindfulness in your daily activities. Whether it's eating, walking, or working, be fully present in the moment. Mindfulness fosters a deeper connection with the spiritual dimensions of your experiences.

8. **Explore Different Spiritual Practices:** - Diversity can be enriching. Explore various spiritual practices, traditions, or philosophies. You may discover aspects that resonate deeply with your soul, contributing to a more holistic spiritual growth.

9. **Be Open to Change:** - Spiritual growth often involves transformation. Be open to change, even if it feels uncomfortable initially. Sometimes, the most significant growth emerges from periods of transition.

10. **Listen to Your Inner Wisdom:** - Trust your intuition and inner wisdom. Your heart often knows the path you need to take. Take moments of silence to listen and connect with the deeper aspects of yourself.

11. **Practice Self-Compassion:** - Spiritual growth involves self-discovery, and this journey may uncover both light and shadows within. Practice self-compassion, understanding that imperfections are part of the human experience.

12. **Express Gratitude:** - Cultivate a spirit of gratitude. Acknowledge and appreciate the blessings in your life. Gratitude opens your heart to the abundance of the present moment.

Remember, the journey of spiritual growth is unique to each individual. May you find inspiration, wisdom, and a profound sense of peace as you navigate the path towards a more spiritually balanced and fulfilling life.

C. Closing Thoughts on the Sacred Journey of Sexuality

As we conclude our exploration of the sacred journey of sexuality, it's essential to reflect on the profound insights gained and consider the transformative nature of this exploration. Here are some closing thoughts:

1. **Embracing Sacredness:** - Recognize the inherent sacredness within the realm of sexuality. The intimate connection between partners is not only physical but a manifestation of a deeper, spiritual union.

2. **Balancing Passion and Reverence:** - Strive for a harmonious balance between passion and reverence. The fiery passion of physical intimacy can coexist with a deep respect for the sacred essence of sex.

3. **Seeking Spiritual Connection:** - Understand that sexual experiences can be a gateway to spiritual connection. When approached with mindfulness and a recognition of the divine within each other, these moments become profoundly sacred.

4. **Navigating Challenges with Wisdom:** - Challenges within the realm of sexuality are part of the human experience. Approach them with wisdom, seeking guidance from spiritual principles, and using them as opportunities for growth and understanding.

5. **Honoring Individual Journeys:** - Every individual's journey of sexuality is unique. Choose to honor and respect diverse perspectives, experiences, and expressions of intimacy, understanding that the sacred journey is deeply personal.

6. **Fostering Open Communication:** - Cultivate open and honest communication with your partner about the sacred nature of your sexual connection. Shared understanding and mutual respect create a foundation for a spiritually enriching journey together.

7. **Practicing Mindful Intimacy:** - Infuse mindfulness into moments of intimacy. Be fully present, appreciating the spiritual connection that unfolds during these shared experiences.

8. **Continual Exploration:** - View sexuality as a continual exploration of the self and your connection with a partner. The sacred journey unfolds over time, revealing new dimensions and insights with each step.

9. **Celebrating Divine Union:** - Celebrate the divine union that occurs when two individuals come together intimately. It is not only a physical joining but a spiritual communion that transcends the boundaries of the self.

10. **Acknowledging Growth and Transformation:** - Embrace the growth and transformation that the sacred journey of sexuality brings. For as long as the individuals and partners evolve, so too does the depth and richness of the spiritual sacred connection within intimate relationships.

In conclusion, the sacred journey of sexuality is a profound odyssey that encompasses the physical, emotional, and spiritual dimensions of human connection. May this exploration inspire a deeper understanding, appreciation, and reverence for the sacred essence that permeates the intimate relationships we share.

Don't miss out!

Visit the website below and you can sign up to receive emails whenever Sophia Mcintyre publishes a new book. There's no charge and no obligation.

https://books2read.com/r/B-A-EYJDB-EDMWC

Also by Sophia Mcintyre

REMOTE MASTERY - UNLEASHING PRODUCTIVITY IN A HOME-OFFICE ENVIRONMENT
Seven Effective and Practical Ways to Engage in Prayer.
Loyalty to God: A Journey into the Depths of Faithfulness, Allegiance and Devotion.
Sacred Union: Exploring the Spiritual Dimensions of Sex and Its Impact on the Soul.